2nd Edition

Washington
Real Estate Laws & Rules

Washington Real Estate Laws and Rules

Executive Editor: Sara Glassmeyer

Project Manager: Elizabeth King, KnowledgeWorks Global Ltd

Product Specialist: Deborah Miller

Cover Designer: Brian Brogaard

Cover Image: Alexander Kirch / EyeEm

Copyright © 2021 Mbition LLC

ALL RIGHTS RESERVED. No part of this work covered by the copyright herein may be reproduced, transmitted, stored, or used in any form or by any means graphic, electronic, or mechanical, including but not limited to photocopying, recording, scanning, digitizing, taping, web distribution, information networks, or information storage and retrieval systems, except as permitted under Section 107 or 108 of the 1976 United States Copyright Act, without the prior written permission

> For product information and technology assistance, contact us at
> **Mbition Customer Support, 800-532-7649.**
> For permission to use material from this text or product, please contact publishingsupport@mbitiontolearn.com.

Library of Congress Control Number: 2018967169
ISBN-13: 978-1-62980-952-6
ISBN-10: 1-62980-952-7

Mbition, LLC
18500 W Corporate Drive, Suite 250
Brookfield, WI 53045
USA

Visit us at **www.mbitiontolearn.com**

Printed in the United States of America
1 2 3 4 5 23 22 21 20 19

Chapter 1
Real Estate License Law and Regulations I 1

Chapter 2
Real Estate License Law and Regulations II 25

Chapter 3
Real Estate License Law and Regulations III 41

Chapter 4
Washington Laws 69

Index 87

Real Estate License Law and Regulations I

CHAPTER 1

 **OVERVIEW**

This lesson identifies the licensing law and regulations to which real estate licensees must adhere. Requirements to obtain, maintain, and renew licenses are detailed.

 **OBJECTIVES**

Upon completion of this lesson, the student should be able to:

1. identify state and local agencies offering assistance to consumers in real estate transactions
2. identify real estate business activities or professions in Washington where one is required to hold a broker's license and identify which government agency has oversight of those activities or professions where such a license is not required
(e.g., title work, property management, mortgage broker, etc.)
3. describe the general purposes of real estate license law
4. explain how license laws/statutes and administrative rules are created and describe the differences between them
5. describe the powers and duties of the Director of the Department of Licensing
6. describe the powers and duties of the Real Estate Commission

7. explain the different types of licensees, including broker, managing broker, designated broker, and branch manager
8. identify the real estate activities that require a license
9. identify the persons exempt from the license requirement to manage real property
10. describe the general licensing and application procedures for brokers and managing brokers
11. explain the continuing education requirements and renewal process for all Washington licensees

State and Local Regulation

(http://access.wa.gov/)

The state of Washington and its governmental agencies have a tremendous effect on real property.

Various state agencies play a role in protecting consumers in real estate transactions. Among these agencies are:

- the Human Rights Commission, which ensures that persons are not discriminated against in residential real estate transactions
- the Department of Ecology and the Environmental and Land Use Hearings Office, among others, which deal with environmental issues
- the Attorney General's Office, which enforces the Unfair Business Practices – Consumer Protection Act
- the Department of Licensing, which ensures that persons in the real estate and appraisal businesses are licensed and regulated
- the Department of Financial Institutions, which regulates mortgage brokers and companies, consumer lending companies, and escrow companies
- the Department of Labor and Industries, which regulates and licenses contractors

License	Regulator
Appraiser	Department of Licensing
Mortgage loan originator	Department of Financial Institutions
Escrow	Department of Financial Institutions
Title insurance	Office of the Insurance Commissioner
Contractors	Department of Labor and Industries

Local units of government may establish statutory law through orders of the various boards of county commissioners or the ordinances of city councils. Many of these laws, such as those that involve zoning, subdivision ordinances, health codes, building codes, and sign codes, have a direct effect on the use of real property.

Laws passed by the Washington Legislature and signed into law by the governor are collected and published as the **Revised Code of Washington** (RCW). Typically, an appropriate state agency is given authority to create rules necessary to carry out the laws. The rules generally expand upon the statutes, providing greater specificity and detail. In Washington, these administrative rules are collected and published as the **Washington Administrative Code** (WAC).

State Real Estate Regulation

To protect the public from the risks involved when unqualified agents negotiate real estate transactions, the Legislature created (or **promulgated**) a law requiring the licensing of real estate agents. It is found in RCW 18.85, and it provides the general standards for the acceptable performance of real estate brokerage services.

The rules and regulations relating to real estate licensees are created by the **Director of the Department of Licensing** (the Director), with the advice and approval of the **Real Estate Commission** (the Commission). These are contained in WAC 308-124. They provide specific criteria for adhering to the standards set in the statute. Although not actually law, these rules have the same force and effect as the law. A violation of a rule is a violation of the law.

Department of Licensing

DIRECTOR OF LICENSING [RCW 18.85.041, .075]

The Director administers and enforces the real estate licensing law. **The Director** has the authority to:
- issue, with the Commission's advice, rules governing the licensing and activities of real estate licensees, including:
  - the licensing of persons licensed in other states
  - criminal background checks for applicants
  - permissible forms of advertising

- enforce all laws and rules relating to real estate licensing and real estate education, including:
  - granting or denying real estate licenses
  - holding hearings
  - fixing the times, places, and method of holding license exams
- institute educational programs for licensees and colleges
- certify prelicensing and continuing education courses and schools, including:
  - charging fees for certification
  - taking disciplinary action, including:
    - reprimand or censure
    - suspension, withdrawal, or denial of certification issuance or renewal
    - fines of up to $5,000 per violation

To avoid any conflict of interest, the Director and employees of the **Department of Licensing** (the Department, or DOL) who administer real estate laws or rules cannot have any financial interest in any real estate business regulated by the law. In addition, any real estate licensee employed by the state must place his/her license on inactive status.

REAL ESTATE COMMISSION [RCW 18.85.021, .025, .031, .035]

The Commission is an advisory board that meets four times a year or at the call of the Director. It consists of the Director and six commissioners appointed by the governor for six-year terms. At least two commissioners must be from east of the Cascades, and at least two must be from west of the Cascades. The other two can be from anywhere in the state.

To be a commissioner, a person must satisfy one of these requirements:

- have five years of real estate experience in Washington
- have three years of experience in investigative work of a similar nature, preferably in connection with the administration of real estate license law in Washington or another state

The Commission:

- holds real estate education conferences
- advises the Director about the issuance of rules and regulations
- provides criteria for real estate schools and courses
- ensures license exams are prepared and administered at exam centers throughout the state
- approves license exam locations outside the state on occasion
- establishes procedures, adopted into rule by the Director, for licensees to follow in referring home inspectors to potential homebuyers

Neither the Director nor the Commission can get involved in disputes between licensees or between licensees and clients. The function of the Director is to administer the law. The function of the Commission is to advise. The Commission is not responsible for administering the law. Disputes that are not the result of clear violations of the law must be settled either in court or through outside mediation or arbitration.

License Requirement

[RCW 18.85.011(15), .331]
Chapter 18.85 RCW makes it illegal for a person to act as a real estate broker, managing broker, or real estate firm without a license. No person can sue to collect compensation as a real estate licensee without proving that he/she was licensed before he/she offered to perform the service or procured a promise of compensation for the service.

> The term person can apply to:
> - a **natural person** (i.e., an individual)
> - a **business entity** (e.g., a corporation, limited liability company, limited liability partnership, partnership, public or private organization, or entity of any character)

DEFINITIONS

Firm *[RCW 18.85.011(17)]*

A **real estate firm** (or **firm**) is a sole proprietorship, partnership, limited liability partnership, corporation, limited liability company, or other legally recognized business entity that is licensed as a real estate firm by the Department to conduct real estate brokerage services in Washington.

Real Estate Brokerage Services *[RCW 18.85.011(13), (16)]*

Real estate brokerage services are services offered or rendered in one of these ways:

- directly or indirectly to another, or on behalf of another, for compensation or the promise or expectation of compensation
- by a licensee on the licensee's own behalf

> The term **licensee** may refer to any person holding a broker, managing broker, or firm license.

These services include the following:
- listing; selling; purchasing; exchanging; optioning; leasing; renting; or negotiating or offering to negotiate the purchase, sale, exchange, lease, or rental of any of the following:
  - real estate, any real property interest in real estate, or any interest in a cooperative
  - a manufactured or mobile home in conjunction with the purchase, sale, lease, exchange, or rental of the land on which the manufactured or mobile home is or will be located
- advertising or holding oneself out to the public as being engaged in real estate brokerage services

- advising, counseling, or consulting buyers, sellers, landlords, or tenants in connection with a real estate transaction
- issuing a **broker's price opinion** (i.e., an oral or written report of property value that is prepared by a licensee and is not an appraisal)
- collecting, holding, or disbursing funds in connection with negotiating, listing, selling, purchasing, exchanging, optioning, leasing, or renting real estate or any real property interest in real estate
- performing **property management services**, which include:
  - marketing; leasing; renting; or physically, administratively, or financially maintaining real property
  - supervising these activities

Broker [RCW 18.85.011(2); WAC 308-124C-145]

A **real estate broker** is a natural person who, on behalf of a firm, performs real estate brokerage services under the supervision of a designated broker or managing broker. He/She can be licensed to only one firm at any one time and cannot supervise any other licensees.

For the initial two years of licensing, a broker is subject to a heightened degree of supervision, including:

- submitting the following to the designated broker or appointed managing broker:
  - evidence of completion of Department-required education courses
  - brokerage service contracts and documents within five days of a client's signature
- having all required real estate brokerage agreements and services reviewed by the designated broker or appointed managing broker
- securing advice or assistance from the designated broker or appointed managing broker when offering brokerage services beyond the broker's level of expertise

Managing Broker [RCW 18.85.011(14)]

A **managing broker** is a natural person who, on behalf of a firm, performs real estate brokerage services under the supervision of the designated broker and who may supervise other brokers or managing brokers licensed to the firm. Any broker who supervises or exercises a right of control over other brokers in the performance of real estate brokerage services must be licensed as a managing broker. A managing broker can be licensed to only one firm at any time.

Designated Broker [RCW 18.85.011(8), (10), .121; WAC 308-124A-805]

A firm must have a designated broker who is responsible for its activities. A **designated broker** is a natural person who:

- owns a sole proprietorship firm, or
- acts as a designated broker on behalf of a firm that is a legally recognized business entity (e.g., a corporation, limited liability company, limited liability partnership, or partnership real estate firm) with its own **Unified Business Identifier** (UBI).

A designated broker must:

- have a **controlling interest** in the firm (i.e., the ability to control the operational and/or financial decisions of the firm), and
- hold a managing broker's license with a "designated broker" endorsement from the Department. The address on his/her endorsement is the location where he/she is the managing broker.

A designated broker must be registered with the Department. He/She may act as a designated broker for more than one firm, provided he/she immediately notifies the Department of additional firms for which he/she serves as designated broker. The designated broker will receive a printed endorsement on his/her managing broker's license indicating the names of all firms for which he/she serves as designated broker. The Department's Real Estate Program registers the address of each firm from which the designated broker accepts endorsement.

Branch Manager [WAC 308-124-300(1); WAC 308-124C-130]

A **branch manager** is a natural person who holds a managing broker's license and has been delegated authority by the designated broker to manage a single physical location of a branch office. He/She is issued a branch manager endorsement by the Department.

For Example

Rainbow Realty is a limited liability company owned by April Shoughers. As required, April obtains a managing broker's license with an endorsement as a designated broker for the firm.

April then decides to establish a separate firm for commercial real estate. She may be the designated broker for that firm, provided that it has its own Unified Business Identifier, that she notifies the Department of Licensing that she is the firm's designated broker, and that she has her managing broker's license endorsed to show that she is the designated broker for both firms.

If she decides to also become the designated broker for a property management firm owned by another person, she can have her license endorsed to be the designated broker of that firm as well, as long as the businesses are separate entities with their own UBIs.

Branch managers are responsible for overseeing the branch office's licensees, employees, and contractors, including:

- the hiring, transferring, and releasing of licensees to and from the branch
- all activity within the branch office, including the supervision of brokers and managing brokers and the heightened supervision of brokers who have been licensed for less than two years

RESPONSIBILITIES OF LICENSEES [WAC 308-124C-135, -140]

Broker and managing broker licensees are responsible for being appropriately licensed. They must be knowledgeable of the Real Estate Brokers and Managing Brokers Act [RCW 18.85], the Real Estate Brokerage Relationships Act [RCW 18.86], the Uniform Regulation of Business and Professions Act [RCW 18.235], and their related rules. Licensees must ensure that all real estate brokerage services in which they participate are in accordance with these acts.

For Example

Fanny Mack has a real estate broker's license. She cannot perform any real estate brokerage services unless she is doing so on behalf of a real estate firm. She can be licensed only under one firm. For instance, if her firm handles only residential transactions and she wishes to engage in commercial transactions, too, then she cannot engage in residential transactions for one firm and commercial transactions for another. She cannot engage in transactions in Vancouver for one firm and transactions in Spokane for another. She can have her license transferred from one firm to another, but she cannot have licenses to represent two firms at the same time or represent a firm under which she is not licensed while licensed with another.

Fanny must be under the supervision of a designated or managing broker. The fact that she has been licensed for 15 years does not relieve the firm from its responsibility to supervise her performance. As long as she prefers not to satisfy the requirements to become a managing broker, she must be supervised and cannot supervise other licensees.

Fanny Mack's branch manager, Freddy Maye, must hold a managing broker's license in order to supervise Fanny's performance of real estate brokerage services. Like Fanny's broker's license, Freddy's managing broker's license can be held only by an individual, not by a business entity, and it allows Freddy to be licensed to only one firm at a time. Unlike Fanny's license, Freddy's license allows him to supervise and exercise control over other brokers.

Broker and managing broker licensees must keep the Real Estate Program informed of their current mailing address and cooperate with the Department in investigations, audits, or licensing matters.

Brokers [WAC 308-124C-140]

A broker's responsibilities include:

- adhering to licensing laws and rules regarding the following:
  - safe handling of customer or client funds and property
  - timely delivery of transaction documents, brokerage service contracts, and customer or client funds and property
  - proper and legal advertising
  - modifying or terminating brokerage service contracts on behalf of the firm
- following the designated broker's written policy on the referral of home inspectors
- delivering transaction documents and brokerage service contracts to the designated broker or delegated managing broker within two business days of mutual acceptance

Designated Brokers [RCW 18.85.275; WAC 308-124-300, -124C-125]

A designated broker's responsibilities include ensuring that:

- monthly trial balances and reconciliation of trust bank accounts are completed, up-to-date, accurate, and balanced
- policies and procedures are in place to account for safe handling of customer or client funds and property
- the accessibility of the firm's offices and records to the Director's authorized representatives and the availability of copies of required records upon demand
- all persons performing real estate brokerage services on behalf of the firm and the firm itself are appropriately licensed

- **affiliated licensees** (i.e., natural persons licensed as brokers or managing brokers employed by the firm and licensed to represent the firm in the performance of any real estate brokerage services) submit their transaction documents to the designated broker, branch manager, or delegated managing broker within two business days of mutual acceptance

The designated broker can delegate these responsibilities to managing brokers and branch managers. He/She must maintain up-to-date written assignments of delegations for these duties, signed by all parties to the agreements. Delegations must:

- be made only to managing brokers licensed to the firm
- address duties of:
  - record maintenance
  - advertising
  - trust accounting
  - safe handling of customer or client funds and property
  - authority to bind
  - reviewing of contracts
  - modifying or terminating **brokerage service contracts** (e.g., purchase and sale agreements, lease or rental agreements, listings, options, agency agreements, or property management agreements) on behalf of the firm
  - supervision of brokers and managing brokers
  - heightened supervision of brokers who have been licensed for less than two years
  - hiring, transferring, and releasing licensees to or from the firm

A designated broker's responsibilities also include:

- maintaining, implementing, and following a written policy that addresses:
  - referral of home inspectors in compliance with the WAC
  - levels of supervision of all brokers and managing brokers of the firm
  - review of all brokerage service contracts involving any affiliated licensee of the firm licensed for less than two years (This review must be completed by the designated broker or the delegated managing broker within five business days of mutual acceptance, with documented proof of review maintained by the firm at its record locations.)
- providing the Department with a closing firm affidavit within five business days when closing the firm

Managing Brokers and Branch Managers

[WAC 308-124C-130, -137]
Managing brokers' and branch managers' responsibilities include those delegated to them by the designated broker (e.g., ensuring the timely review of contracts, that affiliated licensees are following the designated broker's written policies, that required records are maintained and up-to-date).

As with a designated broker, a branch manager's responsibilities include ensuring:

- the accessibility of the firm's offices and records to the Director's authorized representatives and the availability of copies of required records upon demand
- all persons employed by, contracted by, or representing the firm at the branch location are appropriately licensed
- affiliated licensees are submitting their transaction documents to the designated broker or delegated managing broker within two business days of mutual acceptance

EXEMPTIONS [RCW 18.85.151]

The following persons are exempt from licensing:

- a person who buys or disposes of property and/or a business opportunity for his/her own account (or that of a group of which he/she is a member) and his/her employees
- an attorney-in-fact acting under a power of attorney without compensation
- an attorney-at-law performing his/her law practice
- a receiver; trustee in bankruptcy; executor; administrator; guardian; personal representative; or any person acting under the order of any court, selling under a deed of trust, or acting as trustee under a trust
- an employee of a town, city, county, or governmental entity involved in an acquisition of property for right-of-way, eminent domain, or threat of eminent domain
- a person who, as owner or manager of a self-service storage facility, rents or leases individual storage space
- a person who provides referrals to licensees but is not involved in the negotiation or execution of documents or related real estate brokerage services, and he/she is not compensated contingent upon a licensee's receipt of compensation
- a person who does not promote the purchase, listing, sale, exchange, optioning, leasing, or renting of a specific real property interest, including a/an:
  - certified public accountant
  - natural person or entity (including a title or escrow company, escrow agent, attorney, or financial institution) acting as an escrow agent
  - investment counselor
- a person employed or retained by, for, or on behalf of the owner or a designated or managing broker to perform only the following property management activities:
  - delivering a lease application, lease, or lease amendment to a person
  - receiving a lease application, lease, lease amendment, security deposit, rental payment, or any related payment made payable to the real estate firm or owner

- - showing a rental unit or executing a lease or rental agreement under the direct instruction of the owner or designated or managing broker
  - providing information about a rental unit, a lease, an application for a lease, or a security deposit and rental amounts to a prospective tenant
  - assisting in the performance of property management functions by carrying out administrative, clerical, financial, or maintenance tasks
- office personnel (e.g., a secretary, bookkeeper, accountant, unlicensed personal assistant) who do not engage in real estate brokerage services

PERSONAL ASSISTANTS
[RCW 18.85.411; www.dol.wa.gov/business/realestate/assistants.html]

Many real estate brokers will employ an unlicensed assistant to provide clerical, administrative, and technical support. If an unlicensed assistant performs activity that requires a license, then:

- he/she is guilty of a gross misdemeanor and subject to criminal penalties
- his/her employing broker will be subject to disciplinary sanction for accepting brokerage services performed by an unlicensed person

To avoid this problem, many brokers will hire another licensed broker as a salaried assistant. A broker may choose to act as a licensed assistant so that he/she can limit his/her activities and hours of employment.

COMMERCIAL REAL ESTATE BY OUT-OF-STATE LICENSEES
[RCW 18.85.131]

In Washington, an out-of-state licensee who does not also hold a Washington license may render licensed services for **commercial real estate** (i.e., any real estate other than real estate containing one to four residential units) only if he/she does so under a written cooperation agreement with a licensed Washington designated broker who holds an active managing broker's license. The agreement must include:

- the terms of cooperation
- oversight by the Washington broker
- explanation of compensation
- a statement that the out-of-state licensee and its agents will agree to adhere to Washington laws

The out-of-state licensee must also:

- give the Washington designated broker a copy of his/her current license in good standing from the jurisdiction where he/she maintains an active real estate license
- consent that legal actions arising out of his/her conduct or that of his/her agents may be commenced in any Washington county where the cause of action arises or where the plaintiff resides
- include the name of the Washington broker, managing broker, or firm on all advertising
- deposit all required documentation, records, and documents related to the transaction with the Washington broker, managing broker, or firm to be held for three years

Brain Teaser #1

Complete the following sentences to reinforce your understanding of the material.

1. A designated broker must have a(n) _____ interest in the firm.
2. _____ licensees are natural persons licensed as brokers or managing brokers employed by the firm.
3. Any broker who supervises or exercises a right of control over other brokers in the performance of real estate brokerage services must be licensed as a(n) _____ broker.
4. A broker's _____ is an oral or written report of property value that is prepared by a licensee and is not an appraisal.
5. In Washington, an out-of-state licensee without a Washington license may render licensed services for commercial real estate only if he/she does so under a written _____ agreement with a licensed Washington designated broker.

 ## How to Get a License

BROKER'S LICENSE
[www.dol.wa.gov/business/realestate/brokerslicense.html; RCW 18.85.101]

To get a broker's license, an individual must:

- be at least 18 years of age
- have a high school diploma or its equivalent
- successfully complete 60 hours of an approved Real Estate Fundamentals course and 30 hours of an approved Real Estate Practices course within the two years prior to applying for the license examination
- pay for and pass the broker's license examination
- pay the license fee

MANAGING BROKER'S LICENSE *[RCW 18.85.111; WAC 308-124A-750; www.dol.wa.gov/business/realestate/mngbrokerslicense.html]*

To get a managing broker's license, an individual must:

- be at least 18 years of age
- have a high school diploma or its equivalent
- have at least three years of licensed experience as a full-time real estate broker in Washington (or in another jurisdiction having comparable requirements) within the five years prior to applying for the license examination, or have practical experience in a business allied with or related to real estate

- pay for and pass the managing broker's license examination
- pay the license fee
- within the three years prior to applying for the license examination, successfully complete 90 hours of approved Real Estate Brokerage Management, Business Management, and Advanced Real Estate Law courses. Each course must be at least 30 hours.

> Courses used to satisfy continuing education requirements can be used to satisfy the managing broker prelicensing requirement, provided the applicant passed the course's final exam. Licensees must provide additional approved coursework to satisfy any other continuing education requirements.

FIRM LICENSE
[RCW 18.85.091; www.dol.wa.gov/business/realestate/firmlicense.html]

The applicant for a firm license must provide the Director with:

- an application that includes:
  - the firm's name and UBI number
  - a list of all owners and/or persons with a controlling interest in the firm
  - a Washington business mailing and street address, any contact telephone number, and a mailing and physical address for the firm's trust account and/or business records location
- any internet homepage site and business e-mail address
- business papers, including:
  - a copy of the firm's master business license
  - documents supporting the firm's business structure (e.g., articles of incorporation, partnership agreement, certificate of authority, certificate of formation, etc.)
  - the current license of the incoming designated broker
- a Real Estate Endorsement Application (form RE-620-016) for each branch manager or designated broker
- a license fee

To receive a firm license, the firm must:

- not adopt a name that is the same or similar to currently issued licenses or that implies the firm is a nonprofit, a research organization, or a public or governmental agency
- ensure that no person with controlling interest in the firm is the subject of a final Department order suspending or revoking any type of real estate license
- provide the Director with the name of any owners or others with a controlling interest in the firm and designate a managing broker as the designated broker with authority to act for the firm; both the firm and the designated broker must pay a license and license renewal fee

CHARACTER [RCW 18.85.171; WAC 308-124A-700]

A license applicant must also provide the Director with proof concerning his honesty, truthfulness, and good reputation. Proof of the identity of the applicant or the officers or partners of a firm making the application must also be provided. This may include fingerprints and background checks.

A fingerprint card is required from an applicant applying for his/her first:

- Washington broker's license
- managing broker's license using alternative qualifications

Unless the applicant is a corporation or a limited liability company, the applicant must submit fingerprints and a fee for a fingerprint-based background check to the Director for processing through the Washington State Patrol Criminal Identification System and the Federal Bureau of Investigation. The Director may consider the recent issuance of a license or recent employment in a position that required a fingerprint-based national criminal information background check to accelerate the licensing and endorsement process.

An application that is submitted without the required fingerprint card is considered incomplete.

If a fingerprint card is rejected, an applicant must pay a new fee for fingerprinting and background processing and submit a new fingerprint card to the Department within 21 days of written notice to the address of record with the Real Estate Program.

EXAM AND EDUCATION [WAC 308-124A-705, -707]

To take a broker's license examination, an applicant must:

- contact the testing service at least one day prior to the desired test date to schedule and pay for an exam; if requesting a morning or afternoon exam, he/she will be scheduled immediately for the exam and be provided a registration number confirming the reservation
- on the day of the exam, submit to the testing service a completed examination application and any supporting documents, including evidence for completion of a 60-hour Fundamentals course and a 30-hour Practices course approved by the Real Estate Program

The applicant will be charged the full exam fee if he/she does not:

- provide two days' notice to the testing service prior to changing the scheduled examination date
- arrive and take the exam at the time it was scheduled or rescheduled

Clock Hours [RCW 18.85.141; WAC 308-124A-755, -835]

A person desiring to take a broker's or managing broker's license examination who received clock hours in another jurisdiction must:

- submit to the Real Estate Program proof of education to be substituted for the clock hours required (After receiving a written notice that the qualifications for the examination have been verified by the Department, he/she may contact the testing service at least one day prior to the desired test date to schedule and pay for an exam.)

- on the day of the exam, provide a completed exam application to the testing service

The Director may allow substitution of the clock hours for a person who provides a transcript showing completion of equivalent coursework in an institution of higher education or a degree-granting institution (e.g., a person who obtained a law degree or real estate associate degree from a college). The Department may require certification from an authorized representative of the institution that the coursework satisfies the Department's prescribed course content or curriculum for the course.

A course completed in another jurisdiction may be approved for clock hour credit if:

- the course was offered by a tax-supported, public technical, or community college, or any other institution of higher learning, and the Director determines it substantially satisfies the general requirements for course approval
- it was approved to satisfy an education requirement for real estate licensing or renewal and offered by an entity approved to offer the course by the real estate licensing agency in that jurisdiction
- the Director determines that the course substantially satisfies the general requirements for course approval

Prior Licensure [WAC 308-124A-720]

An exam applicant who can present to the Department a license verification form from the real estate regulatory authority in another jurisdiction showing he/she is or was within the past six months actively licensed in good standing in that jurisdiction does not need to satisfy any Washington prelicensing education requirements or take the national portion of the license exam.

After receiving notification that his/her qualifications for the exam have been verified by the Department, the applicant can contact the testing service to schedule and pay for an exam. He/She must submit the approved examination application and any supporting documents required by the Department when he/she arrives for the exam. A person licensed as the equivalent of a managing broker in another jurisdiction is eligible for either a managing broker's or a broker's license.

The Director may consider entering into written recognition agreements with other jurisdictions that license brokers and managing brokers similarly to Washington. These agreements require the other jurisdiction to grant the same licensing process to Washington licensees as Washington does to applicants from the other jurisdiction.

The Exam [WAC 308-124A-710, -765]

An applicant who does not qualify on the basis of a license elsewhere must take the entire license exam and pass both the national portion and the state portion. These exam portions are graded separately. An applicant who passes one portion and fails the other needs to retake only the part he/she failed and pass it within six months. There is no limit to the number of times he/she may

> **FOR EXAMPLE**
>
> When Blossom took her real estate broker's exam, she passed the national portion but failed the state portion. She retook the state portion twice more in the next five months but did not pass.
>
> On her next attempt, eight months after she had passed the national portion, she passed the state portion. However, because she had not passed both parts within six months, she had to retake the national portion, too. Four months later, she passed the national portion.
>
> Thirteen months from the second time she passed the national portion, she applied for her license. She was told she was one month too late and needed to retake the national and state portions of the broker's exam. Because she had completed her prelicensing education more than two years earlier, she was told she needed to take her education over, too.
>
> Blossom decided to pursue another career.

retake an exam. However, if the applicant has not passed both parts within six months, he/she must retake the entire exam to qualify for licensing.

Examination results are valid for only one year. A person who does not become licensed within one year from the date of passing a broker's or managing broker's examination must take and pass another exam in order to become licensed.

EXPERIENCE [WAC 308-124A-713, -715]

An applicant for a managing broker's license who is not currently actively licensed or was not licensed elsewhere within the past six months must provide the Department with the following:

- a copy of his/her high school diploma or its equivalent
- proof of three years of actual experience as a full-time real estate licensee in Washington or elsewhere within the past five years

> **Full-time experience** means the applicant spent at least 40 hours per week in licensed activity or derived a major portion of his/her income from licensed activity during the three-year period.

A person without three years of experience as a licensee may qualify for a managing broker's license by obtaining a waiver based on practical experience in a business allied with or related to real estate. Qualifying experience is any of the following within the past seven years:

- postsecondary education with a real estate major together with one year of experience:
    - as a real estate broker
    - as an attorney with practice in real estate transactions
    - in a field related to real estate
- five years of experience:
    - with decision-making responsibility in closing real estate transactions for an escrow company, lending institution, etc.
    - as an officer of a lending institution or title company involving all phases of real estate transactions

- as a fee appraiser or salaried appraiser for a governmental agency
- in all phases of land development, construction, financing, selling, and leasing of residences, apartments, or commercial buildings
- in real estate investment, property management, or analysis of investments or business opportunities

The Director may grant a waiver upon receipt of an exam application accompanied by a letter requesting the waiver and providing:

- a detailed personal history or work resume
- supporting documentation
- a letter from five business associates describing, from personal knowledge, the applicant's qualifications and experience

A waiver is valid for one exam. An applicant with a waiver who fails the managing broker's exam loses the waiver and must satisfy the experience requirement to qualify for re-examination.

APPLICATION [WAC 308-124A-725, -727]

A person who wishes to be licensed as a real estate broker or managing broker, or endorsed as a branch manager or designated broker, must apply on a form approved by the Director. The broker's and managing broker's application must be signed by the designated broker to whom the license will be issued. The branch manager may sign for the designated broker for the licenses to be issued to that branch office.

The application serves as an interim license for up to 45 days (until the license is issued or denied), unless grounds exist to take disciplinary action against the license. Interim licenses are available only for the broker's license. A broker applicant may begin working on or after the date the following are postmarked or hand-delivered to the Department:

- the notice of passing the examination
- the license application form
- a fingerprint card
- license and fingerprint fees

License Expiration and Renewal

RENEWAL [RCW 18.85.191; WAC 308-124A-735]

An individual's real estate license first issued before July 1, 2010 expires on the licensee's birthday every two years. An individual license issued after June 30, 2010 expires every two years on the date of issuance.

A firm license also expires every two years from the date of its issuance or, in the case of a legally recognized business entity, earlier if the registration or certificate of authority filed with the Secretary of State expires.

The license expiration date is also considered the renewal date.

Firm License [RCW 18.85.091; WAC 308-124A-740]

The following must be provided to the Department for renewal of a firm license:
- renewal fee
- notice of any change in the:
    - controlling interest for the firm
    - firm's registration or certificate of authority filed with the Secretary of State
- proof of a current master business license renewed by the Secretary of State if the firm is a corporation

Individual License [RCW 18.85.101; WAC 308-124A-785]

To renew a license for an individual, a broker or managing broker must complete continuing education courses and pay a renewal fee.

A fingerprint card and background check is required for every active renewal every six years. An application submitted without the required fingerprint card is considered incomplete. If a fingerprint card is rejected, the applicant must pay a new fee for fingerprinting and background processing and must submit a new fingerprint card to the Department within 21 days of written notice to the address of record with the Real Estate Program. If a licensee fails to submit a new fingerprint card, then his/her license will be suspended until the Department receives the fingerprint card.

CONTINUING EDUCATION [RCW 18.85.211; WAC 308-124A-790]

A broker or managing broker applying for renewal of an active license must submit evidence that he/she has completed at least 30 clock hours of real estate instruction in real estate courses approved by the Real Estate Program, subject to the following restrictions:

- Courses may be started only after issuance of a first license and within 48 months of the licensee's renewal date.
- A minimum of 15 clock hours must be completed within 24 months of the licensee's current renewal date (i.e., up to 15 clock hours of instruction in excess of the 30 clock hours submitted for one license renewal may be used for credit for the next renewal).
- At least three of the 15 hours completed within the current renewal period must be in "current issues in Washington real estate" (residential, commercial, or property management), either as a separate course or within another course.
- For the first renewal of a broker's license, the licensee must complete 90 hours that consist of 30-hour courses in Real Estate Law and Advanced Practices and 30 hours of continuing education courses.

Approved courses may be repeated for continuing education credit in subsequent renewal periods. Clock hour credit for continuing education will not be accepted for a course that was:

- not approved
- taken to activate an inactive license
- used to satisfy the requirements for:
    - a real estate broker or managing broker's license
    - reinstatement

Instructors may not receive clock hour credit for teaching or course development. In order to prevent a licensee from placing a license on inactive status to avoid the continuing education or postlicensing requirements, a licensee must:

- submit evidence he/she has completed the continuing education necessary to activate a license if activation occurs within one year after it had been placed on inactive status and the last license renewal had been as an inactive license
- submit evidence he/she has completed any postlicensing requirements not previously satisfied upon returning to active status

LATE RENEWAL [WAC 308-124A-780]

A renewal application may be submitted up to one year after the license expiration date by paying an additional penalty fee. After one year, the license is canceled. However, a person may have a license reinstated within two years after its cancellation by satisfying either of the following options:

1. submit an application to the Director providing proof of:
   - successful completion, within one year before the application, of 60 clock hours of approved real estate coursework (with at least 30 clock hours in the broker's Real Estate Law course)
   - payment of all back renewal fees and penalty fees
   - payment of a reinstatement penalty fine of $100
2. satisfy the procedures and qualifications for initial licensing, including successful completion of:
   - any applicable licensing examinations
   - required broker or managing broker courses, whichever are applicable, within the three years before the application

Once the license has been canceled beyond two years, the former licensee will have to satisfy requirements for initial licensing in order to become licensed again.

Brain Teaser #2

Complete the following sentences to reinforce your understanding of the material.

1. To qualify for a managing broker's license, a person must have _____ year(s) of licensed experience and _____ hour(s) of additional education.

2. A broker's application serves as an interim license for up to _____ day(s) (until the license is issued or denied).

3. A fingerprint card and background check is required for every active renewal every _____ year(s).

4. A renewal application may be submitted up to _____ year(s) after the expiration date by paying an additional penalty fee.

5. Once a license has been canceled beyond _____ year(s), the former licensee will have to satisfy requirements for initial licensing to become licensed again.

Brain Teaser Answers

Brain Teaser #1

1. A designated broker must have a **controlling** interest in the firm.

2. **Affiliated** licensees are natural persons licensed as brokers or managing brokers employed by the firm.

3. Any broker who supervises or exercises a right of control over other brokers in the performance of real estate brokerage services must be licensed as a **managing** broker.

4. A broker's **price opinion** is an oral or written report of property value that is prepared by a licensee and is not an appraisal.

5. In Washington, an out-of-state licensee without a Washington license may render licensed services for commercial real estate only if he/she does so under a written **cooperation** agreement with a licensed Washington designated broker.

Brain Teaser #2

1. To qualify for a managing broker's license, a person must have **three** years of licensed experience and **90** hours of additional education.

2. A broker's application serves as an interim license for up to **45** days (until the license is issued or denied).

3. A fingerprint card and background check is required for every active renewal every **six** years.

4. A renewal application may be submitted up to **one** year after the expiration date by paying an additional penalty fee.

5. Once a license has been canceled beyond **two** years, the former licensee will have to satisfy requirements for initial licensing to become licensed again.

Review — Real Estate License Law and Regulations I

This lesson identifies the licensing law and regulations to which real estate licensees must adhere. Requirements to obtain, maintain, and renew licenses are detailed.

Various state agencies play a role in protecting consumers in real estate transactions. Among them are the Human Rights Commission, the Department of Ecology, the Environmental and Land Use Hearings Office, the Attorney General's Office, the Department of Licensing, the Department of Financial Institutions, and the Department of Labor and Industries.

To protect the public from the risks involved when unqualified agents negotiate real estate transactions, the Legislature created a law requiring the licensing of real estate agents. It is found in Chapter 18.85 of the Revised Code of Washington (RCW). The rules and regulations relating to real estate licensees are created by the Director of the Department of Licensing (the Director). These are contained in Washington Administrative Code (WAC) 308-124. Although not actually law, these rules have the same force and effect as the law.

The Director administers and enforces the real estate licensing law. The Director has the authority to issue, with the Commission's advice, rules governing the licensing and activities of real estate licensees; enforce all laws and rules relating to real estate licensing and real estate education; institute educational programs for licensees and colleges; and certify prelicensing and continuing education courses and schools.

Chapter 18.85 RCW makes it illegal for a person to act as a real estate broker, managing broker, or real estate firm without a license.

A real estate broker is a natural person who, on behalf of a firm, performs real estate brokerage services under the supervision of a designated broker or managing broker. For the initial two years of licensing, a broker is subject to a heightened degree of supervision. A managing broker is a natural person who, on behalf of a firm, performs real estate brokerage services under the supervision of the designated broker and who may supervise other brokers or managing brokers licensed to the firm.

A real estate firm must have a designated broker who is responsible for its activities. This is a natural person who owns a sole proprietorship firm or is designated to act as a designated broker on behalf of a firm that is a legally recognized business entity. He/She must have a controlling interest in the firm and hold a managing broker's license with a "designated broker" endorsement from the Department of Licensing (the Department, or DOL).

A branch manager is a natural person who holds a managing broker's license and has been delegated authority by the designated broker to manage a single physical location of a branch office. Branch managers are responsible for overseeing the branch office's licensees, employees, contractors, brokers, managing brokers, and the heightened supervision of brokers who have been licensed for less than two years.

Broker and managing broker licensees are responsible for being appropriately licensed. They must be knowledgeable of pertinent laws and rules relating to real estate and must ensure that all real estate brokerage services in which they participate are in accordance with them. They must keep the Real Estate Program informed of their current mailing address and cooperate with the Department in investigations, audits, or licensing matters. Brokers must follow the written policy on the referral of home inspectors.

A designated broker's responsibilities include ensuring the firm's compliance in matters such as trust accounts and customer funds, managing the accessibility of records to the Director and licensing of employees; maintaining up-to-date written assignments of delegations of managing broker and branch manager duties; and maintaining, implementing, and following a written policy that addresses referrals of home inspectors, levels of supervision within the firm, and review of brokerage services contracts.

Managing brokers' and branch managers' responsibilities include those delegated to them by the designated broker. A branch manager's responsibilities are similar to those of a designated broker and also include following and implementing the designated broker's written policy.

Exemptions from licensing law include: a person who buys or disposes of property for his/her own account or for a group of which he/she is a member; an attorney-in-fact acting under a power of attorney without compensation; an attorney-at-law in performing his law practice; any person acting under the order of any court or acting as trustee; an employee of a town, city, county, or governmental entity involved in an acquisition of property for right-of-way or eminent domain; an owner or manager of a self-service storage facility renting or leasing individual storage space; a certified public accountant, escrow agent, or investment counselor if he/she does not promote the purchase, sale, or rental of a specific real property interest; and an employee performing only certain property management activities.

Licensing requirements for brokers include being at least 18 years of age; having a high school diploma or its equivalent; successfully completing 90 hours of approved real estate courses within the two years prior to applying for the license examination; paying for and passing the broker's license examination; and paying the license fee.

To qualify for a managing broker's license, applicants must have at least three years of licensed experience and 90 hours of additional education. A person without three years' experience as a licensee may qualify for a managing broker's license by obtaining a waiver based on practical experience in a business allied with or related to real estate. An applicant for a firm license must provide the Director with an application form, a license fee, and formation and business documents.

A license applicant must also provide the Director with proof concerning his honesty, truthfulness, and good reputation. Proof of the identity of the applicant, the officers, or the partners of a firm making the application must also be provided. This may include fingerprints and background checks. A broker application serves as an interim license for up to 45 days (until the license is issued or denied), unless grounds exist to take disciplinary action against the license.

An individual's real estate license first issued before July 1, 2010 expires on the licensee's birthday every two years. One issued after June 30, 2010 expires every two years on the date of issuance. A firm license also expires every two years from the date of its issuance or, in the case of a legally recognized business entity, earlier if the registration or certificate of authority filed with the Secretary of State expires.

A firm renewing a license must provide a renewal fee; notice of any change in the controlling interest of the firm, the firm's registration, or certificate of authority; and, if a corporation, proof of renewal of its current master business license. To renew a license for an individual, a broker or managing broker must complete continuing education courses and pay a renewal fee.

A renewal application may be submitted up to one year after the expiration date by paying an additional penalty fee. After one year, the license is canceled. However, a person may have a license reinstated within two years after its cancellation either by submitting proof of completing 60 approved education hours and paying certain fees and penalties or by satisfying the procedures and qualifications for initial licensing.

This concludes the review for Real Estate License Law and Regulations I.

Real Estate License Law and Regulations II

CHAPTER 2

This lesson identifies requirements for operating a real estate firm in the state, including the requirements for licensee supervision and recordkeeping. Grounds for and types of disciplinary actions are discussed.

Upon completion of this lesson, the student should be able to:

1. describe the basic office requirement for operating a real estate company in Washington
2. explain the role of the managing broker regarding supervision of affiliated licensees
3. describe the required procedures when a licensee leaves a brokerage firm voluntarily and when a managing broker terminates a licensee
4. identify and describe the major grounds for disciplinary action against licensees
5. describe the procedures outlined in the license law that address disciplinary actions

Real Estate Firm Requirements

NAMES [RCW 18.85.221; WAC 308-124A-815]

A license authorizes only the person named on it to perform licensed activity, and the licensed person can only perform licensed activities under the name that appears on the license. A real estate firm, however, does have the option to use one or more assumed names in the conduct and operation of its real estate business, provided it obtains a separate license for each additional assumed name. All real estate brokerage services must be conducted in the firm's name or in one of its licensed assumed names.

A licensee also can operate and advertise only under his/her own name, unless the Director gives written consent for use of another name (e.g., an individual licensee who is generally known under a nickname and wishes to use that nickname for general business purposes).

The **Department of Licensing** (the Department, or DOL) can deny, suspend, or reject a firm name or assumed name that, in the Department's opinion:

- is derogatory
- is similar or identical to another licensed firm name
- implies that the firm is a public or government agency
- implies that the firm is a nonprofit or research organization

A firm cannot advertise using names or trade styles that would be rejected for any of the above reasons.

A bona fide franchisee may be licensed using the name of the franchisor (e.g., Century 21) along with the firm name of the franchisee.

OFFICES [RCW 18.85.231; WAC 308-124B-200, -205, -207; WAC 308-124D-225]

Every firm must have an office or records depository in Washington accessible to the Director's representatives. Firms must maintain and produce required records.

The office may be at a location where the designated broker also conducts a separate business activity, provided the brokerage business activities and records are kept separate from the other business activities.

The licenses of the real estate brokers and real estate managing brokers must be available at the address appearing on the individual license. All firm and branch office licenses must be displayed in an area visible to the public. Every office must display the name of the firm as licensed at the address on the license, which should also be visible to the public.

Within 10 days of when a licensee changes its office address, the designated broker must submit to the Real Estate Program:

- a completed change-of-address application
- completed transfer applications
- all licenses, with fees for their reissuance, for persons licensed at that office

Branch Offices [RCW 18.85.241]

A designated broker may establish one or more branch offices under the firm's name after completing the following:

- paying a license fee
- obtaining a duplicate license for each branch office

The duplicate license shows the locations of the main office and that branch. It must be displayed in the branch office.

Each branch office must have a managing broker authorized by the designated broker to perform the duties of a branch manager. The branch manager is responsible for all brokers licensed to work in that office. A branch office cannot legally operate without a branch manager.

A branch office license is not needed where real estate sales activity is conducted at one particular subdivision or tract if the main office or another branch office is located within 35 miles of it.

Offices for Brokers Actively Licensed in Another Jurisdiction [WAC 308-124D-220]

A broker who is actively licensed in another jurisdiction in which his/her headquarters office is located satisfies the requirement for having an office in Washington if he/she:

- has a Washington location where he/she maintains trust account and transaction records that are:
  - open and accessible to Department representatives
  - maintained for at least three years
  - accessible to the parties for which they were prepared or retained
- notifies the Department of the address where the records are maintained in Washington and includes this address with the headquarters office address on the license application
- posts the Washington license at this location

A firm seeking licensure in Washington whose headquarters office is licensed in another jurisdiction must:

- obtain a firm license
- register a natural person who qualifies as a managing broker in Washington and has a controlling interest in the firm to be the firm's designated broker in Washington

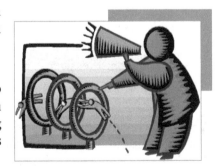

If a licensee receives a notice of audit, then he/she must go to the Department office nearest to the location of the records (i.e., Olympia or Seattle) to sign the audit report within 30 days of the mailing. An appointment must be made in advance to sign the audit report.

SUPERVISION [RCW 18.85.081, -.275, -.361]

Listings, transactions, management agreements, and other contracts related to providing brokerage services are the property of the real estate firm. With regard to funds and records required to be held or maintained by the real estate firm:

- a broker must timely deliver them to the appointed managing broker
- the managing broker is responsible for them only after they are received from the broker and must timely deliver them to the designated broker
- the designated broker is responsible for them only after they are received from the managing broker or broker

A designated broker:

- may delegate, in writing, to a managing broker licensed to the firm the duties of:
  - safe handling of client funds
  - maintenance of trust accounts and records of transactions and trust accounts
  - supervision of brokers
- must keep a record of the firm's managing brokers and their delegations
- has the authority to accept new or transferred licensees to represent the real estate firm

A designated broker or managing broker:

- has the authority to amend, modify, bind, create, rescind, terminate, or release real estate brokerage service contracts on behalf of the real estate firm
- must supervise the conduct of brokers and managing brokers in their performance of real estate brokerage services and provide a heightened level of supervision during the first two years of a broker's licensure

Grounds for which disciplinary action can be taken against a real estate firm and/or a managing or designated broker include:

- failing to exercise adequate supervision over the activities of brokers and managing brokers within the scope of the license law
- accepting the services of, or continuing in a representative capacity, any broker or managing broker:
  - who has not been granted a license
  - after his/her license has been revoked or during a license suspension
- failing to preserve records relating to any real estate transaction for the three years following the submission of the records to the firm

A person who is employed by and conducts real estate transactions on behalf of a town, city, or county may hold an active real estate license. If he/she does, then his/her designated and managing brokers are not responsible for his/her real estate transactions on behalf of the town, city, or county employer.

MAINTENANCE AND RETURN OF LICENSE
[RCW 18.85.291; WAC 308-124A-730;
http://www.dol.wa.gov/business/realestate/brokersupdate.html]

A person licensed as a broker or managing broker may perform duties and activities only as a representative of the firm and only under the direction and supervision of a licensed managing broker, branch manager, or designated broker. His/Her license must be kept by the firm. When a licensee ceases to represent the firm, his/her license will no longer be in force.

License Surrender

Either the broker, managing broker, branch manager, or designated broker may unilaterally terminate his/her licensed relationship at any time through written notice by the:

- designated broker to the broker, managing broker, or branch manager
- broker, managing broker, or branch manager to the designated broker or the designated broker's delegated representative

The firm, through the managing broker, branch manager, or designated broker, must then give notice of termination to the Real Estate Program without delay and surrender the licensee's license. The managing broker, branch manager, or designated broker may not condition the license's surrender upon the performance of any act by the broker or managing broker.

If the license cannot be surrendered because the managing broker or designated broker is placing conditions upon the surrender of it:

- the licensee must inform the Department of this in writing
- upon receiving the written statement, the Real Estate Program will process the release or license transfer

The termination date is the postmark date, the fax date, or the date the license is hand-delivered to the Real Estate Program.

If the license cannot be surrendered to the Real Estate Program because it has been lost, then the licensee and the responsible managing broker, branch manager, or designated broker must submit a letter of release.

License Transfer

No license transfer is permitted unless the license is surrendered or a letter of release is submitted and filed with the Real Estate Program. A broker or managing broker may transfer to another firm only after he/she:

- pays a transfer fee
- obtains a new license for the unexpired term of the surrendered license

Termination for Violation

If the firm terminates a broker's or managing broker's services for a violation of license law, the Real Estate Brokerage Relationships Act, or the Uniform

Regulation of Business and Professions Act, then the designated broker must immediately file a written statement of the facts with the Director.

Firm Closing [WAC 308-124A-30]

When a firm closes, the designated broker is responsible for providing the Department with a closing firm affidavit.

Change of Designated Brokers [WAC 308-124A-825]

When a firm changes designated brokers, a license will not be issued for a new designated broker unless the outgoing and incoming designated brokers submit to the Department a signed statement that:

- lists all outstanding client trust liabilities and pending transactions
- certifies sufficient funds are in trust to meet client trust liabilities

Reversion from Managing Broker to Broker License
[WAC 308-124A-726]

A managing broker may revert from a managing broker to a broker by completing department forms and paying the required fees. If the managing broker is in an active status, then the designated broker must sign the forms.

To revert back again to a managing broker, the broker will have to meet all current statute requirements, including taking the examination.

INACTIVE LICENSES [RCW 18.85.265]

Whenever a license is returned to the Director, it becomes an inactive license. A person holding an inactive license cannot conduct real estate brokerage services. However, he/she is subject to denial, suspension, or revocation of the license as a penalty for violation of the real estate law.

After the license becomes inactive, the licensee may apply and pay a fee to:

- have a new active license issued for the unexpired term of his/her license
- renew the license as an inactive license, without any continuing education
- have a new active license issued within one year after placing the license on an inactive status and renewing it as an inactive license, showing completion of continuing education requirements
- have a new active license issued more than three years after the license was made inactive, in which case he/she must complete an approved 30-hour real estate course within the 12 months prior to applying for an active license

If no Department background check was conducted within the last six years, then a new background check is required to activate the license.

If any proceedings to suspend or revoke the license have been started, then an inactive license cannot be changed to an active license until the proceedings are completed.

Brain Teaser #1

Complete the following sentences to reinforce your understanding of the material.

1. A branch office cannot legally operate without a branch _____.
2. Listings, transactions, management agreements, and other contracts related to providing brokerage services are property of the real estate _____.
3. When a firm closes, the designated broker is responsible for providing the Department a closing firm _____.
4. When a licensee ceases to _____ a firm, his/her license will no longer be in force.
5. Whenever a license is returned to the Director, it becomes a(n) _____ license.

 Records

DELIVERY OF FUNDS AND RECORDS

[RCW 18.85.285; WAC 308-124C-105, -110; WAC 308-124E-100]

An affiliated licensee (i.e., a broker or managing broker) must deliver or transmit complete copies of all transaction records and brokerage agreements, and he/she must physically deliver all funds, negotiable instruments, or items of value to the appropriate managing broker, branch manager, or designated broker:

- within two **business days** (i.e., days other than Saturdays, Sundays, or legal holidays)
- sooner, if the terms of the client/customer contract necessitate quicker delivery

The designated broker must keep adequate records of all real estate transactions handled by or through any firms to which he/she is registered. These records, which must be open to inspection by the Director or his/her authorized representatives, include:

- an accurate, up-to-date log of all agreements or contracts for brokerage services submitted by the firm's affiliated licensees
- a legible copy of the transaction or contracts for brokerage services
- a transaction folder containing all agreements, contracts, documents, leases, closing statements, and correspondence for each:
    - real estate or business opportunity transaction
    - rental, lease, contract, or mortgage collection account
- for sales transactions, a copy of the purchase and sale agreement, the earnest money receipt, an itemization of the receipts and disbursements, the final settlement statement, and any addenda related to the accounting or disposition of client funds kept in the same office where the trust account records are kept

The designated broker is also required to keep the following trust account records:

- duplicate receipt book or a cash receipts journal that records all receipts
- sequentially numbered, nonduplicative checks with a check register, cash disbursements journal, or check stubs
- validated duplicate bank deposit slips or daily verified bank deposit
- client's accounting ledger summarizing all moneys received and all moneys disbursed for each:
  - real estate or business opportunity transaction
  - property management account, contract, or mortgage collection account
- separate ledger sheets for each tenant (including security deposit), lessee, vendee, or mortgagor; for automated systems, the ledger sheets may be a computer-generated printout that contains required entrees
- reconciled bank statements and canceled checks for all trust bank accounts

A designated broker must preserve records relating to any real estate transaction and have them available for inspection by the Director or his/her representatives for at least three years following its consummation. All required records must be maintained at a location where the firm is licensed. This location may be the main office or any branch office.

However, once a transaction has been closed for a year, its files may be stored at a single remote facility in Washington, provided that the broker:

- maintains a list at his/her licensed location identifying the records at the facility
- immediately retrieves requested records upon demand by a Department representative

Transaction records may be stored on permanent, non-erasable storage media, such as optical disc or microfilm, provided:

- the storage media is indexed in a way to allow for immediate retrieval of all documents
- the retrieval process does not permit modification of the documents
- equipment is maintained in good repair at the broker's licensed location so transaction documents can be viewed and printed
- the records are available upon demand by a Department representative at the broker's licensed location

All records must be accurate, posted, and kept up-to-date. The designated broker is responsible for:

- the custody, safety, and correctness of entries on all required records, even if other persons actually prepare, keep, or record the entries
- ensuring that the office and records are accessible to Department auditors (He/she must provide copies of required records to the Director or his/her representatives upon demand.)

Both the firm and its designated broker are responsible for recordkeeping. When the designated broker is replaced, and the outgoing designated broker and incoming designated broker sign the statement certifying that funds in the trust account are adequate to meet the firm's client trust liabilities, the incoming designated broker is not responsible for any discrepancy identified in the statement unless he/she contracts to accept that responsibility.

ELECTRONIC COMMUNICATIONS
(www.dol.wa.gov/business/realestate/docs/REnewsltr-winter2014.pdf)

Electronic communications, such as e-mail, are used by licensees to receive and send copies of contracts, disclosures, and other important documents and information from and to various parties of the transaction. Like all other documents and writing obtained or executed by a licensee in connection with a transaction, electronic communications must be maintained by the firm as part of the transaction file.

Electronic communications can be key to proving whether a licensee disclosed a material fact or provided a required disclosure. Retaining and maintaining them can reduce a licensee's need to defend unwarranted allegations.

Real estate firms should have written office policies and procedures to govern how electronic communications are created, sent, or received in connection with a brokerage services transaction.

Disclosures
[WAC 308-124C-115]

A licensee must:

- keep the Director informed of his/her current mailing address
- regardless of any pending appeal, notify the Real Estate Program within 20 days after service or knowledge of:
  - any criminal complaint, information, indictment, or conviction (including a plea of guilty or nolo contendere) in which the licensee is named as a defendant
  - entry of a civil court order, verdict, or judgment against the licensee involving any real estate- or business-related activity by the licensee
- upon demand, disclose any information or produce any document, book, or record in his/her possession for inspection by the Director or his/her representatives

Enforcement

The Director has authorization to enforce the laws under the license law as well as the Uniform Regulation of Business and Professions Act.

VIOLATIONS AND SANCTIONS [RCW 18.85.361, -.411; RCW 18.235 110, -.130]

The Uniform Regulation of Business and Professions Act allows the Director to sanction licensees and license applicants for the following acts, which constitute unprofessional conduct:

- misrepresenting or concealing a material fact in obtaining or reinstating a license
- false, deceptive, or misleading advertising
- incompetence, negligence, or malpractice resulting in harm or damage to a consumer or an unreasonable risk of harm or damage to a consumer
- failing to adequately supervise staff to the extent that consumers may be harmed or damaged
- professional license suspension, revocation, or restriction in another jurisdiction
- failing to comply with an order
- violating a lawful rule
- helping an unlicensed person to engage in real estate practice
- practicing or operating a profession beyond the scope of his license
- misrepresentation in the conduct of his/her practice
- conviction of (or a plea of guilty or nolo contendere to) a gross misdemeanor or felony relating to his/her practice
- committing any act involving moral turpitude, dishonesty, or corruption relating to the practice of real estate
- registration as a sex offender
- failing to cooperate in an investigation, audit, or inspection by not:
  - furnishing requested papers, documents, or a requested written explanation
  - responding to a subpoena
  - providing Department representatives conducting an investigation, inspection, or audit with access to facilities
- interfering with an investigation or disciplinary action by:
  - willfully misrepresenting facts
  - using threats, harassment, or financial inducements to prevent or attempt to prevent a consumer or witness from providing evidence

Each of the following is considered a gross misdemeanor, for which the violator can be criminally prosecuted:

- obtaining or attempting to obtain or maintain a license by misrepresentation or fraudulent representation
- acting as a broker, managing broker, or real estate firm without a license
- violating any provision of the law

The Director has the authority to investigate the actions of any licensee, whether the transaction was for the licensee's own account (e.g., his/her own property) or in his/her capacity as a licensee. The Director may do so because of a verified written complaint or without such a complaint.

If the law or rules are violated, then the Director may:

- hold hearings
- issue a cease-and-desist order
- obtain an injunction
- censure or reprimand the licensee

- require satisfactory completion of a specific program of remedial education
- require compliance with conditions of probation for a designated period
- monitor and/or restrict or limit the licensee's practice
- suspend or revoke the violator's license
- deny an initial or renewal license application
- fine a violator up to $5,000 per violation
- take other corrective action

If any of these sanctions are imposed, then the Director may require the violator to reimburse the Department for investigative costs. All money received from fines is held in a Real Estate Education Program account in the custody of the State Treasurer, for use in education programs conducted by the Department for licensees.

If a designated broker loses his/her license, the licenses of *all affiliated licensees* will no longer be in effect until they can find a new designated broker.

HEARINGS AND APPEALS
[RCW 18.85.380, -.390; RCW 18.235.050; RCW 34.05.467]

When the Director determines that a violation of the law may have occurred, he/she may prepare and serve a statement of charges accompanied by a notice that a hearing to contest the charges may be requested within 20 days after being served.

If no hearing is requested, the Director may enter a decision based on the available facts. If a hearing is requested, the time of the hearing must be fixed as soon as convenient, but no earlier than 30 days after service of charges unless a summary suspension or summary restriction has been issued.

The hearing officer must keep a transcript of the proceedings and furnish a certified copy to the accused licensee or applicant upon request.

If the Director finds that a statement or accusation is not proved after considering the evidence, then he/she will dismiss the case. If the Director decides the evidence supports the accusation, he/she may enter an order imposing sanctions. The order takes effect immediately upon being served, but the licensee may, within 10 days of the service of a final order, file a petition for reconsideration or stay.

Within 30 days from the date of the Director's decision, the licensee may appeal in the Superior Court by filing with the court clerk a $1,000 cash bond to the state of Washington to pay all costs that may be awarded against him/her if he/she loses.

When appealed, an order is not stayed unless the Director or the Court enters an order staying it.

CEASE-AND-DESIST ORDERS [RCW 18.85.390; RCW 18.235.150]

If the Director finds that the public interest will be irreparably harmed by delay in issuing an order, then he/she may issue a temporary cease-and-desist order, which may become permanent and include a civil fine after a hearing or if no hearing is requested.

The licensee may request a hearing be held within 30 days after the request (unless the licensee requests a later hearing) to determine whether the temporary cease-and-desist order should be continued or modified, until another hearing is held to determine whether the order will become permanent.

The Director may issue a notice of intent to issue a cease-and-desist order to stop a person from engaging in the unlicensed practice of real estate. That person then has 20 days after service of the notice to request an adjudicative proceeding to contest the allegations. If the Director makes a final determination that the person did engage in unlicensed activity, then the Director may:

- issue a permanent cease-and-desist order
- impose a civil fine not exceeding $1,000 for each day of violation

OTHER DISCIPLINARY MEASURES [RCW 18.85.420, -.430]

The Director may also exercise any of the following:

- sue in Superior Court to get an injunction to stop a person from violating the law
- petition the Court to immediately appoint a receiver to take over, operate, or close a real estate office violating the law, pending a hearing
- refer a complaint for violation of any section of the license law before a court

In any legal action taken against violators of the law, and in any appeals, the Director will be represented by the Prosecuting Attorney of the county in which the violation occurred. If the Prosecuting Attorney fails to act, then the Director may have the State Attorney General represent him.

> The Attorney General is the Director's legal advisor and acts as his/her attorney in all actions and proceedings brought by or against him/her.

Any process issued by the Director may be served by an authorized process server or may be mailed by certified mail with a return receipt requested to the licensee's last business address of record in the Director's office.

Washington Center for Real Estate Research [RCW 18.85.471]

The **Washington Center for Real Estate Research** (WCRER) was created in 1989 by the Board of Regents at Washington State University to provide credible research, value-added information, education services, and project-oriented research to real estate licensees, real estate consumers, real estate service providers, institutional customers, public agencies, and communities in Washington and the Pacific Northwest.

The WCRER may exercise any of the following:

- conduct studies and research on:
  - affordable housing and strategies to meet the state's affordable housing needs
  - real estate and urban or rural economics and economically isolated communities
- disseminate its findings of real estate research
- supply research results and educational expertise to the Real Estate Commission
- prepare information of interest to real estate consumers and make the information available to the general public, universities, colleges, and appropriate state agencies
- encourage economic growth and development in Washington
- support the professional development and continuing education of Washington licensees
- study and recommend changes in state statutes relating to real estate
- develop a vacancy rate standard for low-income housing in the state

Brain Teaser #2

Complete the following sentences to reinforce your understanding of the material.

1. An affiliated licensee must deliver complete copies of all transaction records and brokerage agreements and must physically deliver all funds to the appropriate managing broker, branch manager, or designated broker within _____ business day(s) or sooner if the terms of the client/customer contract necessitate quicker delivery.

2. A designated broker must preserve records related to any real estate transaction and have them available for inspection by the Director or his/her representatives for at least ___ year(s) following its consummation.

3. A licensee must notify the Real Estate Program within _____ day(s) after service of a criminal complaint in which the licensee is named as a defendant.

4. The Director may prepare and serve a statement of charges, accompanied by a notice that a hearing to contest the charges may be requested within _____ day(s) after being served.

5. A licensee may appeal the Director's decision in the Superior Court, by filing with the court clerk a $_____ cash bond to pay all costs that may be awarded against him/her if he/she loses.

Brain Teaser Answers

Brain Teaser #1

1. A branch office cannot legally operate without a branch **manager**.

2. Listings, transactions, management agreements, and other contracts related to providing brokerage services are property of the real estate **firm**.

3. When a firm closes, the designated broker is responsible for providing the Department a closing firm **affidavit**.

4. When a licensee ceases to **represent** a firm, his/her license will no longer be in force.

5. Whenever a license is returned to the Director, it becomes an **inactive** license.

Brain Teaser #2

1. An affiliated licensee must deliver complete copies of all transaction records and brokerage agreements and must physically deliver all funds to the appropriate managing broker, branch manager, or designated broker within **two** business days or sooner if the terms of the client/customer contract necessitate quicker delivery.

2. A designated broker must preserve records related to any real estate transaction and have them available for inspection by the Director or his/her representatives, for at least **three** years following its consummation.

3. A licensee must notify the Real Estate Program within **20** days after service of a criminal complaint in which the licensee is named as a defendant.

4. The Director may prepare and serve a statement of charges, accompanied by a notice that a hearing to contest the charges may be requested within **20** days after being served.

5. A licensee may appeal the Director's decision in the Superior Court, by filing with the court clerk a **$1,000** cash bond to pay all costs that may be awarded against him/her if he/she loses.

Review — Real Estate License Law and Regulations II

This lesson identifies requirements for operating a real estate firm in the state, including the requirements for licensee supervision and recordkeeping. Grounds for and types of disciplinary actions are discussed.

A license authorizes only the person named on it to perform licensed activity and only under the name appearing on the license. A real estate firm, however, has the option to use one or more assumed names in the conduct and operation of its real estate business, provided it obtains a separate license for each additional assumed name. An individual licensee may operate and/or advertise only under his/her own name, unless the Director gives written consent to use another name.

Every firm must have an office or records depository in Washington accessible to the Director's representatives. Firms must maintain and produce required records. A designated broker may establish one or more branch offices under the firm's name after paying a license fee and obtaining a duplicate license for each branch office. Each branch office must have a managing broker authorized by the designated broker to perform the duties of a branch manager.

Listings, transactions, management agreements, and other contracts related to providing brokerage services are the property of the real estate firm. Funds and records required to be held or maintained by the real estate firm must be timely delivered by a broker to the appointed managing broker. The managing broker is responsible for them only after they are received from the broker, and he/she must timely deliver them to the designated broker. The designated broker is responsible for them only after they are received from the managing broker or broker.

A person licensed as a broker or managing broker may perform duties and activities only as a representative of the firm and only under the direction and supervision of a licensed managing broker, branch manager, or designated broker. His/Her license must be kept by the firm. When a licensee ceases to represent the firm, his/her license will no longer be in force. The broker, managing broker, branch manager, or designated broker may unilaterally terminate his/her licensed relationship at any time through written notice. The firm must then give notice of termination to the Real Estate Program without delay and surrender the licensee's license.

Whenever a license is returned to the Director, it becomes an inactive license. A person holding an inactive license cannot conduct real estate brokerage services. However, he/she is still subject to denial, suspension, or revocation of the license as a penalty for violation of the real estate law.

An affiliated licensee must deliver or transmit complete copies of all transaction records and brokerage agreements and must physically deliver all funds, negotiable instruments, or items of value to the appropriate managing broker, branch manager, or designated broker within two business days or, if the terms of the client/customer contract necessitate quicker delivery, sooner.

A designated broker must preserve records related to any real estate transaction and have them available for inspection by the Director or his/her representatives for at least three years following its consummation. All required records must be maintained at a location where the firm is licensed.

A licensee must keep the Director informed of his/her current mailing address. He/She must also notify the Real Estate Program within 20 days after service or knowledge of any criminal complaint, indictment, or conviction in which the licensee is named as a defendant or within 20 days of the entry of a civil court order, verdict, or judgment against the licensee involving any real estate- or business-related activity. The licensee must also, upon demand, disclose any information or produce any document, book, or record in his/her possession for inspection by the Director or his/her representatives.

The Director has authorization to enforce the laws under the license law and the Uniform Regulation of Business and Professions Act. The Act allows the Director to sanction licensees and license applicants for acts that constitute unprofessional conduct, including misrepresenting or concealing a material fact in obtaining or reinstating a license; false, deceptive, or misleading advertising; incompetence, negligence, or malpractice resulting in harm or damage to a consumer; professional license suspension or revocation in another jurisdiction; violating an order or rule; helping an unlicensed person to engage in real estate practice; practicing a profession beyond the person's license scope; conviction of a professionally related gross misdemeanor or felony; registration as a sex offender; and failing to cooperate in an investigation, audit, or inspection.

If the law or rules are violated, then the Director may hold hearings; issue a cease-and-desist order; obtain an injunction; censure or reprimand the licensee; require satisfactory completion of a specific program for remedial education; require compliance with conditions of probation for a designated period; monitor and/or restrict the licensee's practice; suspend or revoke the violator's license; deny an initial or renewal license application; fine a violator up to $5,000 per violation; or take other corrective action.

When the Director determines that a violation of the law may have occurred, he/she may prepare and serve a statement of charges accompanied by a notice that a hearing to contest the charges may be requested within 20 days after being served. If no hearing is requested, then the Director may enter a decision based on the available facts. If the Director finds that the public interest will be irreparably harmed by delay in issuing an order, then he/she may issue a temporary cease-and-desist order, which may become permanent and include a civil fine after a hearing or if no hearing is requested.

The Washington Center for Real Estate Research (WCRER) was created in 1989 by the Board of Regents at Washington State University to provide credible research, value-added information, education services, and project-oriented research to real estate licensees, real estate consumers, real estate service providers, institutional customers, public agencies, and communities in Washington and the Pacific Northwest.

This concludes the review for Real Estate License Law and Regulations II.

Real Estate License Law and Regulations III

CHAPTER 3

OVERVIEW

This lesson explains the professional responsibilities related to activities involving licensees in real estate transactions. This includes property management and the handling of clients' trust funds. Agency disclosure requirements and duties are also reviewed.

OBJECTIVES

Upon completion of this lesson, the student should be able to:

1. describe requirements imposed on licensees in presenting written offers, handling private transactions, and presenting disclosures
2. explain in which cases a real estate licensee might need to involve another practitioner rather than perform the function himself/herself
3. describe the purpose of a broker's trust account and explain depositing requirements and disbursement procedures
4. explain the various elements of a property management agreement outlined in the Washington Administrative Code
5. discuss agency disclosure requirements identified in the Revised Code of Washington and the Washington Administrative Code

Transactions

ADVERTISING *[RCW 18.85.361(2); WAC 308-124B-210;WWW.DOL.WA.GOV/ BUSINESS/REALESTATE/ADVERTISING.HTML]*

A licensee is required to disclose his/her license status in any form of advertising utilized. All advertising or solicitations for brokerage services (including internet-based advertising, web pages, e-mail, newspapers, and other visual media) must include the firm's name or an assumed name as licensed, except for ads for personally owned property.

A licensee is prohibited from making, printing, publishing, or distributing false statements, descriptions, or promises that would reasonably induce a person to act if the licensee knew or could reasonably have known of their falsity. He/She is also prohibited from causing, authorizing, or knowingly permitting the making, printing, publication, or distribution of such statements.

Although not every false statement made by a licensee in a real estate transaction is necessarily actionable, the licensee is under a strict duty to exercise reasonable care and inquiry to determine the truth of any material statements, descriptions, or promises that are to be distributed to the public through multiple listing services, advertisements, or any other written or oral public communications.

Internet Advertising and Social Media *(www.dol.wa.gov/business/realestate/docs/SocialMediaGuidelines.pdf)*

All internet-related advertising that consumers can view or experience as a separate unit (e.g., an e-mail message or web page) requires full disclosure, which can be either:

- **licensed firm disclosure**, containing the firm's name or assumed name as licensed or registered with the **Department of Licensing** (the Department, or DOL)
- **licensee disclosure**, containing the following:
  - name of the licensee as shown on his/her Department-issued license
  - registered name or assumed name of the firm in which the licensee is affiliated as registered with the Department

The disclosure is not applicable once an agency relationship has been established with a buyer or seller.

When there is a consumer complaint involving such disclosures, the burden of proof falls on the licensee, the firm, and the designated broker.

All statutes and rules regarding advertising apply equally to the internet. This includes websites, e-mail, and other potential online identification, representation, promotion, or solicitation to the public that is related to licensed real estate activity. Compliance with Washington state guidelines does not ensure compliance with other jurisdictions' guidelines, laws, or regulations.

OFFERS [RCW 18.85.285; RCW 18.86.030]

Licensees must deliver (or have delivered) each purchase and sale agreement, listing agreement, and any other similar instrument to all parties signing them within a reasonable time after signing. This generally means:

- the buyer must get a copy after he/she signs the offer
- the seller must get a copy after he/she signs his/her acceptance
- the buyer must get a second copy after the seller signs his/her acceptance
- a copy must be kept in each participating broker's files

When negotiating a sales agreement, the licensee must present all written offers to the seller until a sale closes.

DISCLOSURES [RCW 18.85.361; RCW 18.86.030]

A licensee must make certain disclosures in a transaction, including:

- providing a pamphlet on the law of real estate agency to all parties to whom he/she renders real estate brokerage services before the party:
  - signs an agency agreement with him/her
  - signs an offer in a real estate transaction handled by him/her
  - consents to dual agency
  - waives any rights
- before a party signs an offer in a real estate transaction handled by him/her, disclosing in writing to all parties to whom he/she renders real estate brokerage services whether he/she represents the buyer, the seller, both parties, or neither party; the disclosure must be in one of the following, in a separate:
  - paragraph titled "Agency Agreement" in the agreement between the buyer and the seller
  - writing titled "Agency Agreement"
- if accepting anything other than cash or its equivalent as earnest money (e.g., a promissory note), communicating this fact to the seller prior to acceptance of the offer and indicating it on the earnest money receipt
- disclosing his/her license status in writing when buying, selling, or leasing any interest in real property, either directly or through a third party
- if he/she will charge or accept compensation from more than one party in the transaction, disclosing this fact in writing to all parties in the transaction
- disclosing any commission, rebate, or direct profit he/she will take, accept, or charge on expenditures made for his/her principal
- disclosing to his/her principal any expectation of receiving a kickback or rebate before directing a transaction involving the principal to a lender or escrow company

LIMITING ACTIVITIES TO AREAS OF COMPETENCE

There are many instances in which a licensee might need to involve another practitioner rather than perform the function himself/herself. For example, the licensee may prepare a competitive market analysis but not an appraisal. He/She cannot call his/her analysis an appraisal, nor will his/her analysis be accepted as an appraisal by a lender.

In trying to conclude a transaction successfully, a licensee may be tempted to go beyond his/her area of expertise. A real estate agent has a duty to advise his/her client (i.e., the seller, the buyer, or both the seller and the buyer if he/she is a dual agent) to seek expert advice on matters relating to the transaction that are beyond the agent's expertise.

In general, a buyer's agent is perhaps more likely than a seller's agent to try to provide advice in areas beyond his/her level of expertise. This is because a buyer might be less experienced than a seller. The buyer has more of a need for inspections; tax advice; and advice on how to hold title, develop land, and interpret restrictions and title reports. A real estate broker has no authorization by virtue of his/her license to act as his/her client's attorney, tax advisor, home inspector, subdivision expert, etc. Legal and tax advice and property inspections are beyond the scope of his/her competency. The broker must recognize when competent legal or other technical advice is required, and he/she must recommend the use of a specialist in situations that would be in his/her principal's best interests.

In a matter such as taxes, agents often walk a fine line. Some tax consequences are so widely known to real estate agents (e.g., the $500,000 exemption on the sale of a home), that the agent not only can, but should, provide the information to his/her principal. However, the agent should also suggest that the principal speak to an expert. The information the real estate agent provides may be accurate, but it may result in the wrong decision for the client, especially if the client is not presented with other aspects of the matter that are less well-known.

This would be particularly true in regard to tax and legal consequences of holding title under one tenancy or another. Although an agent is expected to know the difference between a tenancy in common and a joint tenancy in general terms, the agent should never discuss these matters in specific terms with a principal. Such a discussion would constitute legal advice and could lead to a wrong and costly decision.

A broker may also want to seek the assistance of another broker with transactions in which the broker increases his//her liability beyond acceptable limits. In the following instances, a broker might decide it is better to have another broker represent a party in a transaction than to attempt to represent both parties or deal with an unrepresented party:

- A broker is asked to negotiate a transaction on behalf of a client with another party who has no representation. In assisting the unrepresented party, he/she may unintentionally give the impression that he/she is an agent of that party. This would create an implied agency and, therefore, a dual agency. Without having obtained authorization

from all parties to create a dual agency, he/she would be in violation of license and agency laws.
- When a broker does have dual agency authorization, he/she may find it difficult to represent both parties impartially, particularly if he/she has had a personal or business relationship with one of them.
- In a transaction in which he/she is negotiating on his/her own behalf to buy or sell real estate, a licensee may be exposed to greater liability because of the requirement that he/she deal honestly and in good faith with the other party.

GENERAL CONDUCT [RCW 18.85.341 -.351, -.361; WAC 308-124D-210]

Grounds for the suspension or revocation of a real estate license include:

- engaging in any conduct in a transaction that demonstrates bad faith, dishonesty, untrustworthiness, or incompetence
- failing to perform all acts required by a real estate agreement as quickly as possible or intentionally or negligently delaying performance
- making or knowingly or negligently allowing the making of material false statements, descriptions, or promises that would reasonably induce a person to act
- knowingly committing or being a party to any material fraud, misrepresentation, concealment, conspiracy, collusion, trick, scheme, or device whereby any other person lawfully relies upon the word, representation, or conduct of the licensee

> A licensee must be careful in making any statements regarding the condition or quality of any property being shown so these statements do not become grounds for a lawsuit for damages based on fraudulent misrepresentations.

A licensee cannot misrepresent membership in any state or national real estate association (e.g., call himself/herself a Realtor® if he/she is not a member of the National Association of Realtors®).

A license will be immediately suspended if the **Department of Social and Health Services** (DSHS) certifies that the licensee is not in compliance with a support order or a residential or visitation order. It can be reinstated when the DSHS issues a release stating the licensee is in compliance.

A license will also be suspended for nonpayment or default on a federal- or state-guaranteed educational loan or a service-conditional scholarship until steps are taken to cure the default under a repayment agreement.

If the Director issues a written order objecting to a selling plan on the basis that it endangers the public, then the licensee must stop selling or operating according to the plan. The licensee must obey any cease-and-desist order issued by the Director. If he/she fails to obey the order, then there may be disciplinary action taken.

DISCRIMINATION [RCW 49.60.180, -.222, -.223]

A licensee cannot discriminate against any person in sales activity on the basis of sex, marital status, sexual orientation, race, creed, color, national origin, familial status, military status, or disability or violate any provisions of state or federal anti-discrimination law. On these bases, he/she cannot:

- refuse to engage in a real estate transaction with a person
- refuse to submit a person's written offer to the owner of listed property
- refuse to negotiate the sale or rental of real property to a person
- discriminate against a person in the terms, conditions, privileges of sale or rental of real property, or furnishing of services or facilities
- make or have made any statement indicating an intent to make a preference, limitation, or discrimination with respect to a prospective real estate transaction
- represent that property is not available for inspection, sale, or rental when in fact it is

A licensee also cannot discriminate on these bases in the hiring of a person, along with the additional basis of age.

A licensee cannot engage in **blockbusting** (i.e., inducing persons to sell or rent real property through representations regarding the entry or prospective entry into a neighborhood of persons of a particular race, color, creed, sex, age, national origin, marital status, or familial status or with a sensory, mental, or physical disability).

CLOSINGS [WAC 308-124D-205]

In every real estate or business opportunity transaction in which he/she provides brokerage services, a licensee must ensure the buyer and seller are each furnished with a complete detailed closing statement as it applies to that party at the time the transaction is closed. The licensee's firm must retain a copy of the closing statement even if the licensee does not handle the funds and the closing is done elsewhere.

The closing statements in which a firm participates must show:

- date of closing
- total purchase price
- itemization of all adjustments, money, or things of value received or paid, showing:
  - to whom each item is credited or debited
  - dates of adjustments
  - names of payees, makers, and assignees of all notes paid, made, or assumed

COMMISSIONS [RCW 18.85.301]

No part of a commission for brokerage services or other compensation can be paid by:

- a licensed firm, broker, or managing broker to any person who performs real estate brokerage services and does not have a real estate license in a U.S. state, U.S. possession, or a foreign jurisdiction with a real estate regulatory program

- a licensed firm to a broker or managing broker not licensed with the firm
- a licensed broker or managing broker to any person, whether licensed or not, except through the firm's designated broker

However, a commission may be shared with a licensed manufactured housing retailer on the sale of personal property manufactured housing sold in conjunction with the sale or lease of land.

APPRAISAL [RCW 18.140.020; RCW 18.85.361]

A licensee may make an appraisal only if he/she is licensed or certified as an appraiser. When making an appraisal or issuing any other report on property, a licensee cannot:

- accept employment or compensation contingent upon reporting a predetermined value
- issue a report on property in which he/she has an interest, unless that interest is clearly stated in the report

MOBILE HOMES [RCW 18.85.361; RCW 46.70.021]

A real estate licensee may not sell mobile homes or travel trailers separate from land unless licensed as a mobile home and travel trailer dealer or broker. A real estate licensee can, however, negotiate the purchase, sale, lease, or exchange of new or used mobile homes when the transaction includes the conveyance of the land on which the mobile home is or will be placed.

A licensee engaging in a real estate transaction involving a mobile home must ensure the title to the mobile home is transferred.

TITLE INSURANCE REFERRALS [RCW 18.85.053]

A real estate licensee or person who has a controlling interest in a real estate firm cannot:

- directly or indirectly give any fee, kickback, payment, or other thing of value to any other licensee as an inducement or reward for placing or referring title insurance business or causing it to be given to a title insurance agent in which he/she also has a financial interest
- solicit and/or accept anything of value from a title insurance company, a title insurance agent, or the employees or representatives of a title insurance company or title insurance agent that these entities are not legally allowed to give to him/her
- prevent or deter a title insurance company, title insurance agent, or their employees or representatives from delivering to a real estate licensee or its employees, independent contractors, and clients printed promotional material concerning only title insurance services, as long as:
  - material is business-appropriate and is not misleading or false
  - material does not malign the real estate licensee or its employees, independent contractors, or affiliates
  - delivery of the materials is limited to the areas of the real estate licensee's physical office reserved for unrestricted public access
  - conduct of the employees or representatives is appropriate for a business setting and does not threaten the safety or health of anyone in the licensee's office

A licensee cannot require as a condition of providing real estate services that a consumer obtain title insurance from a title insurance agent in which the licensee has a financial interest.

HOME INSPECTOR REFERRALS [WAC 308-124C-125]

Each designated broker must establish a written office policy that includes a procedure for referring home inspectors to buyers or sellers. The policy will address the consumer's right to freely pick a home inspector of his/her choice and will prevent any collusion between the home inspector and a real estate licensee.

A licensee who refers to a buyer or seller a home inspector with whom he/she has or has had a relationship (e.g., a business or familial relationship) must fully disclose the relationship in writing before the buyer or seller uses the home inspector's services.

SHORT SALES/LOAN MODIFICATIONS [WWW.DOL.WA.GOV/BUSINESS/REALESTATE/DOCS/SHORTSALES-LICENSEES.PDF]

A **short sale** is a real estate transaction in which the proceeds of the sale will not generate sufficient funds to pay the debts secured by the property and the seller is unable to pay the difference. Any creditors with a security interest in the property must consent to receiving less than they are owed in return for releasing any lien on the property.

The DOL and the **Department of Financial Institutions** (DFI) recognize that short sale providers need specialized expertise. Both departments require that to negotiate short sales, a person must either be a Washington-licensed attorney or have a mortgage loan originator license or real estate license.

Short sales are complicated transactions because they require the seller to negotiate at least two separate agreements. One is the purchase and sale agreement with the buyer. The other is the agreement with the creditor(s) to accept less than the amount owed and secured by the property. The DOL regulates real estate brokerage services related to the purchase agreement between the seller and the buyer. The DFI regulates persons offering loan modification services and the negotiation of reduced loan payoffs with creditors.

A broker representing an owner in a short sale owes the owner the same duties as with any other owner under the license law. A broker should advise a short sale seller to seek appropriate tax, legal, and other professional advice or counsel. In addition, brokers have a duty to all parties to disclose material facts, to deal honestly and good faith, and to exercise reasonable skill and care. It is also important for real estate brokers to keep their designated brokers, branch manager, or managing broker informed about all transactions and report any questionable activity.

Any person who provides; offers to provide; or arranges for others to negotiate, obtain, or arrange a short sale must also comply with Federal Trade Commission rules regarding Mortgage Assistance Relief Services (12 CFR 1015) for required disclosures and limitations on fees and performance representation.

Brain Teaser #1

Complete the following sentences to reinforce your understanding of the material.

1. A licensee is required to disclose his/her _____ status in any form of advertising utilized.

2. When negotiating a sales agreement, the licensee must present all _____ offers to the seller.

3. A license will be _____ suspended if the Department of Social and Health Services certifies that the licensee is not in compliance with a support order.

4. A licensee cannot require as a condition of providing real estate services that a consumer obtain title insurance from a title insurance agent in which the licensee has a(n) _____ interest.

5. Each designated broker must establish a written office policy that includes a procedure for referring _____ _____ to buyers or sellers.

Administration of Trust Funds
[WAC 308-124E-105, -110]

TRUST FUNDS *[RCW 18.85.275, -.361(5); WAC 308-124D-200, -205]*

A designated broker is responsible for the administration of trust funds and accounts. He/She must ensure that his/her affiliated licensees safeguard funds or advance fees received from any principal or any party to a real estate or business opportunity transaction, property management agreement, and contract or mortgage collection agreement by holding them in trust for the purposes of the transaction or agreement.

Unless the principals mutually agree in writing that the deposit is to be paid to the lessor, the seller, or an escrow agent named in the agreement, all checks must be made payable to the real estate firm as licensed if received as:

- earnest money
- security or damage deposits
- rent or lease payments
- contract or mortgage payments on real property or business opportunities owned by clients

The designated broker must retain a copy of the written agreement.

If more than one licensee has been involved in the negotiation of a real estate sales agreement and the purchaser is to deposit funds prior to closing, then the firm first receiving the funds retains custody and is accountable until the funds are distributed or delivered in accordance with written instructions signed by all parties to the transaction. However, all licensees must:

- keep the party to whom they provided brokerage services informed of the earnest money deposit status
- retain and provide copies of receipts to the principals and participating firms

All licensees must keep their own funds physically separated from all moneys collected for clients and being held for disbursement for or to clients, including advance fees being held pending the closing of a real estate sale or transaction. The licensee cannot:

- **commingle** (i.e., mix) funds of clients or customers with his/her own funds
- **convert** any money, contract, deed, note, mortgage, abstract, or other evidence of title delivered to him/her in trust or on condition (This means he/she cannot use these for his/her own benefit or for that of his/her managing broker, real estate firm, or any person not entitled to the benefit in violation of the trust or before the occurrence of the condition. Failure to return any of these within 30 days after the owner is entitled to it and makes demand for it is prima facie evidence of conversion.)

For Example

When Mel Lowe places rent from his own properties, which are not under management contract with his brokerage firm, in his clients' trust account, he is guilty of commingling. When he writes checks for expenses on those properties from the clients' trust account in excess of the amount of his own money in the account (which should not be there in the first place), he is converting funds.

TRUST ACCOUNTS *[RCW 18.85.275, -.285, -.311]*
All real estate transaction funds over which the firm will exercise control must be deposited in one or more separate bank accounts designated as real estate trust fund accounts (i.e., **trust accounts**) in a Washington state **banking institution** (i.e., a bank, savings association, or credit union) insured by the **Federal Deposit Insurance Corporation** (FDIC) or the share insurance fund of the **National Credit Union Administration** (NCUA).

The designated broker is responsible for deposits, disbursements, or transfers of clients' funds received and held in trust.

Bank accounts, deposit slips, checks, and signature cards must be designated as trust accounts in the name or assumed name under which the firm is licensed. Trust bank accounts for real estate sales or business opportunity transactions must be interest-bearing demand deposit accounts.

Pooled Interest-Bearing Accounts

Except for property management trust accounts, the firm must maintain a pooled interest-bearing demand deposit trust account as a Housing Trust Fund account for deposit of trust funds of $10,000 or less.

The designated or managing broker will direct the depository institution to:

- remit to the State Treasurer interest or dividends, net of any reasonable and appropriate service charges or fees (which do not include check printing fees or fees for bookkeeping systems), and the average monthly balance in the account (or as otherwise computed in accordance with an institution's standard accounting practice) at least quarterly. The Treasurer will deposit 75% in the Washington Housing Trust Fund and 25% in the Real Estate Education Program account.
- transmit to the Director of Commerce a statement, with a copy to be transmitted to the depositing person or firm, showing the following:
    o name of the person or entity for whom the remittance is spent
    o rate of interest applied
    o amount of any service charges deducted
    o account balance(s) of the period in which the report is made

The Director of Commerce will forward a copy of the reports to the Department to aid in the enforcement of these requirements.

Money from the Housing Trust Fund and other legislative appropriations is used to finance loans or grant projects that provide housing for persons and families with:

- special housing needs
- incomes at or below 50% of the median family income for the county or standard metropolitan statistical area where the project is located

Money deposited in the Real Estate Education Program account and all money derived from fines is used to carry out the Director's programs for education of real estate licensees, others in the real estate industry, and members of the public. The firm or designated broker may, but is not required to, notify the client of the intended use of the funds.

Other Account Options

A licensee must disclose in writing to a party depositing more than $10,000 that the party may choose between having the funds deposited in one of the following:

- pooled interest-bearing account, if the parties to the transaction agree in writing
- separate interest-bearing trust account on which the interest will be paid to the party; the interest earned or bank fees charged on this account would be posted to that party's individual ledger card

If bank charges or fees exceed the interest earned, causing the balance to be less than the trust account liability, then within one banking day after receipt of notice the designated broker must deposit funds from the firm's business account or other nontrust account to bring the trust account into balance with its outstanding liability. For a separate account, he/she may be reimbursed for these charges by the party depositing the funds, if that party authorized reimbursement in writing. For a pooled account, he/she must absorb the excess bank charges or fees as a business expense.

DEPOSITS

Funds need not be deposited into a trust account in transactions concerning a purchase and sale agreement that instructs the broker to deliver an earnest money check directly to a named closing agent or to the seller.

When a transaction provides for an earnest money deposit/note or other instrument to be held by a party other than the firm, a broker must deliver the deposit to the designated broker or responsible managing broker. The designated broker will have the ultimate responsibility for delivering the funds and for obtaining and placing in the transaction file a dated receipt from the party receiving the funds.

Funds cannot be deposited to a trust account if they:

- do not pertain to a client's real estate or business opportunity sales transaction or are not received in connection with a client's rental, contract, or mortgage collection account
- belong to the designated broker or the real estate firm, except for a minimum amount the firm must keep in the account in order to open it or to keep it from being closed, in accordance with the requirements of the financial institution in which the trust account is maintained

Funds or money received for any reason pertaining to the sale, renting, leasing, or optioning of real estate or business opportunities; contract or mortgage collections; or advance fees must be deposited into the firm's trust account on the next **banking day** (i.e., a day other than Saturday, Sunday, or a legal holiday) following receipt, unless the purchase and sale agreement provides for a deferred deposit or delivery.

An earnest money agreement may provide that a check received as an earnest money deposit is to be held for a specified length of time or until the occurrence of a specific event. If that is the case, then the broker must promptly deposit or deliver funds in accordance with the terms of the purchase and sale agreement. However, cash must be deposited the next banking day.

DISBURSEMENTS

Funds cannot be disbursed from a trust account for the following conditions:

- to pay bank charges, other than charges:
  - that may be deducted from interest-bearing accounts
  - for bank services, checks, or other business overhead expenses of the real estate firm

> Arrangements must be made with the bank to charge these to the firm's regular business bank account or to provide a separate monthly statement of bank charges so that they may be paid from the firm's business bank account.

- without a written release from both the purchaser and seller, in advance of the closing of a real estate or business opportunity transaction or before the occurrence of a condition set forth in the purchase and sale agreement, except:
  - as provided by an agreement that terminates according to its own terms prior to closing without a written release
  - to the escrow agent designated in writing by the parties to close the transaction, at a reasonable time prior to the date of closing in order to permit checks to clear
- for items not pertaining to either of the following:
  - specific real estate or business opportunity transactions
  - rental, contract, or mortgage collection accounts
- when pertaining to a specific real estate or business opportunity transaction or a rental, contract, or mortgage collection account, in excess of the actual amount held in the trust account for that purpose

If trust funds are claimed by more than one party to a real estate transaction, then the designated broker or his/her delegate must promptly provide written notification to all contracting parties of his/her intent to disburse client funds. The notification must include the following:

- names and addresses of all parties to the contract
- amount of money held and to whom it will be disbursed
- a date of disbursement, which must occur no later than 30 days after the notification date

The following are conditions for trust fund disbursements; they must be:

- made by check or electronic transfer
- drawn on the trust account
- identified as to a specific real estate or business opportunity transaction or a collection or management agreement

The following can also be true of trust fund disbursements; they can be made:

- based upon wire transfer receipts only after the deposit has been verified
- by wire transfer if the designated broker:
  - provides a follow-up hard-copy debit memo
  - retains in the transaction file a copy of instructions signed by the owner of these funds that identifies the receiving entity and account number
- by check if:
  - no check numbers on any single trust account are duplicated
  - voided checks are permanently defaced and retained
  - the check number, the amount, the date, the payee, the items covered, and the specific client's ledger sheet debited are shown on the check stub or check register; all data must agree exactly with the check as written

To avoid commingling, a designated broker must arrange with the financial institution that any interest assigned or credited to the firm by written assignment agreement be removed from the trust account and credited to the firm's general account.

Commissions

For each commission earned by the firm for a real estate or business opportunity transaction, a separate check identifying the transaction must be drawn on the trust account and payable to the firm as licensed after the final closing. However, commissions to persons licensed to the firm and business expenses of the designated broker or firm must be paid from the firm's regular business bank account, not from the trust account.

Commissions owed to another firm can be paid from the trust account and must be paid promptly upon receipt of funds. Commissions shared with other firms are a reduction of the gross commissions received.

For Example

Whenever a broker from April Shoughers' firm earns a commission on a listing for her firm, April writes checks from her trust account to her firm and to the cooperating brokerage firm after closing. She then deposits her firm's commission into her business account. From her business account she writes a check to the broker who earned the commission for the firm.

TRUST ACCOUNT ADMINISTRATION

A designated broker is responsible for ensuring trust accounts are properly administered, including:

- properly setting up and reconciling a trust account
- depositing, holding, disbursing, receipting, posting, and recording funds
- accounting to principals
- notifying principals and cooperating licensees of material facts

A designated broker must establish and maintain a system of records and procedures, approved by the Real Estate Program, which provides for an audit trail accounting of all funds received and disbursed. If he/she proposes an alternative system, then he/she must obtain the advance written approval of the Real Estate Program.

If a designated broker has a computer system, then the following must be enacted:

- the computer system must provide for the capability to back up all data files
- the designated broker must maintain receipt, check or disbursement registers or journals; bank reconciliations; and monthly trial balances in printed or electronic formats, available for immediate retrieval or printing upon demand of the Department
- he/she must maintain a printed, dated source document file or index file to support any changes to existing accounting records

All funds must be identified to the account of each individual client. Each deposit must be identified by the source of funds and the transaction to which it applies. Any interest credited to a client's account must be recorded as a liability on the client ledger. All checks or funds received must be identified by the date received and by the amount, source, and purpose on either a cash receipts journal or duplicate receipt retained as a permanent record.

The following ledger sheets must be established and maintained:

- individual client's ledger sheet for each client for whom funds are received in trust that shows all receipts and disbursements, including interest earned or bank fees charged if the account is a separate interest-bearing account for the client
- an "open account" ledger sheet for funds used to open or to keep the trust account from being closed
- a "Housing Trust Account interest" ledger sheet if the account is a pooled interest-bearing account on which, upon receipt of the monthly bank statements, the designated broker will:
  - credit the amount indicated as interest credited
  - debit the amount indicated as paid to the state or as bank fees

Ledger sheet credit entries must show the following:

- date of deposit
- deposit amount
- item covered, including but not limited to "earnest money deposit," "down payment," "rent," "damage deposit," "rent deposit," "interest," or "advance fee"

The debit entries must show the following:

- date of the check
- check number
- amount of the check
- name of payee
- item covered, an entry which may:
  - indicate a code number per chart of accounts
  - be documented in a cash receipts journal, cash disbursements journal, or check voucher

The reconciled real estate trust bank account balance must be equal at all times to the outstanding trust liability to clients and the funds in the "open account" ledger. The balance shown in the check register or bank control account must equal the total liability to clients and the "open account" ledger. The checkbook balance, the reconciliation, and the ledgers (including the clients' ledgers and the "open account" ledger) must be in agreement at all times.

> Account Balance = Liability to Clients + Open Account Funds

The designated broker is responsible for preparation of a monthly trial balance of the clients' ledgers, reconciling the ledgers with both the trust account bank statement and the trust account check register or bank control account. A **trial balance** is a listing of all client ledgers, including the "open account" ledger, showing the owner name or control number, the date of last entry to the ledger, and the ledger balance.

Property Management

The regulatory activities governed by the Washington real estate license law include property management.

PROPERTY MANAGEMENT AGREEMENT [WAC 308-124D-215]

For each property managed, a firm must have, and retain for three years following its termination, a written management agreement signed by the owner and designated broker. The agreement must state the following:

- firm's compensation
- type (i.e., apartments, industrial) and the number of units in the project or, if the project is not residential, its square footage
- whether and for what purposes the firm is authorized to collect and disburse funds
- firm's authorization, if any, to hold security deposits and the manner in which the deposits may be disbursed
- how often summary statements will be furnished to the owner; each owner of property managed by the firm must be provided a summary statement in accordance with the property management agreement, showing on a cash basis:
  - the balance in the owner's account carried forward from the previous summary
  - total rent receipts
  - owner contributions
  - other itemized receipts
  - itemization of all expenses paid
  - the ending balance
  - the number of units rented (or the square footage if the property is not residential)

Any amendment or modification in the property management agreement must be:

- written
- signed by the owner and the designated broker
- retained

All properties rented or leased by the firm must be supported by a written rental or lease agreement.

A firm may provide other services to an owner if the owner:
- receives full written disclosure of:
  - any relationship between the firm and the persons providing the service
  - the fees being charged
- gives the firm his/her permission after receiving the full written disclosure

PROPERTY MANAGEMENT TRUST ACCOUNTS
[WAC 308-124E-115]

A designated broker who manages properties must comply with all rules pertaining to trust accounts, except that funds for property management transactions need not be placed in a pooled interest-bearing account. However, he/she may establish an interest-bearing trust account or dividend-earning investment account for funds of an individual owner according to a written management or directive agreement signed by the owner, provided all interest or earnings accrue to the owner. If all owners assign the interest to him/her, then he/she does not need to establish individual interest-bearing accounts for each owner.

The designated broker may establish an interest-bearing trust account for damage and security deposits received from tenants of residential income properties according to a written management agreement, with the interest paid to the owner, if by written agreement the firm is a designated representative of the owner, lessor, or sublessor under the provisions of the Residential Landlord-Tenant Act.

A designated broker may establish a trust account as a common account (or "clearing account"). However, funds that belong to the licensee or the firm and are related to transactions on properties owned by him/her or by the firm cannot be kept in the account.

Accounting

The property management accounting system must be an accounting of cash received and disbursed. Any other method of accounting offered to owners for their rental properties, units, and/or complexes must be supplementary to the firm's accounting of all cash received and disbursed through the firm's trust account(s). All owners' summary statements must include this accounting.

Deposits and Disbursements

If the account contains security deposits or funds belonging to more than one client, then the designated broker may not preauthorize disbursements or deductions for recurring expenses (e.g., mortgage payments) on behalf of one client.

Property management commissions must be withdrawn from the trust account at least once per month. One check payable to the firm may be drawn to cover fees and commissions from all clients if it is supported by a schedule of commissions identified to each client.

Damage or security deposits cannot be disbursed from the trust account without the written agreement of the tenant until the end of the tenancy, when they are to be disbursed to the persons entitled to them based on the terms of the rental or lease agreement and in accordance with state laws.

When the management agreement between an owner and the firm is terminated, the owner's funds must be disbursed according to the agreement. Funds held as damage or security deposits must be disbursed to the owner or the successor property manager. The tenants must be notified by the disbursing firm in accordance with the provisions of the Residential Landlord-Tenant Act.

Brain Teaser #2

Complete the following sentences to reinforce your understanding of the material.

1. The _____ broker is responsible for deposits, disbursements, or transfers of clients' funds received and held in trust.

2. Trust bank accounts for real estate sales or business opportunity transactions must be interest-bearing _____ deposit accounts.

3. Except for property management trust accounts, the firm must maintain a pooled interest-bearing demand deposit trust account as a Housing Trust Fund account for deposit of trust funds of $_____ or less.

4. Each owner of property managed by the firm must be provided a _____ statement as provided in the property management agreement.

5. Property management commissions must be withdrawn from the trust account at least once _____.

Brokerage Relationships Act
[RCW 18.86.010, -.100]

The **Brokerage Relationships Act** pertains to any **real estate transaction** (i.e., an actual or prospective transaction involving a purchase, sale, option, or exchange of any interest in real property, a business opportunity, or a lease or rental of real property) involving a real estate licensee. A prospective transaction does not exist until a written offer has been signed by at least one of the parties. In the statute, the term buyer refers to a **buyer** or tenant and the term **seller** refers to a seller or landlord.

This law clarifies the duties and obligations of all parties in these transactions. It provides that any licensee who performs brokerage services for a buyer is a buyer's agent unless the licensee:

- has a written agency agreement with the seller or both parties
- has a subagency agreement with the seller's agent (As a **subagent**, a licensee is engaged to act on behalf of a principal by the principal's agent, who has been authorized by the principal in writing to appoint subagents.)
- is the seller or one of the sellers
- has a different written agreement from the parties

Licensees affiliated with the same firm may solely represent a buyer and seller in a transaction, but their designated broker will be a dual agent and must get the written consent of both parties to be a dual agent.

A licensee may be the agent of a party in one transaction and at the same time deal with the party in a nonagent capacity in another transaction.

Whether a licensee is an agent or a nonagent, he/she owes all parties in a transaction the duty to:

- exercise reasonable skill and care
- deal honestly and in good faith
- account in a timely manner for all money and property received
- present all written offers and other written communications in a timely manner, even if the property is subject to an existing contract or the buyer is already a party to an existing contract
- provide a pamphlet on the law of real estate agency, consisting of the entire Brokerage Relationships Law and a cover page, to any party to whom he/she renders services before the occurrence of the earliest of the following events the party exercises:
  - signing of an **agency agreement** (i.e., a listing, a buyer agency agreement, a property management agreement, or any other agency agreement with the licensee)
  - signing of an offer in a real estate transaction handled by the licensee
  - consent to dual agency
  - waiving of any rights under the Brokerage Relationships Act
- before a party signs an offer, disclose in a separate paragraph in the sale or lease agreement, or a separate writing called "Agency Disclosure," whether he/she represents the buyer, the seller, both parties, or neither
- disclose all known material facts not apparent or readily ascertainable to a party

> A material fact is information that:
> - substantially adversely affects the property value or a party's ability to perform its obligations in a transaction
> - materially impairs or defeats the purpose of the transaction
>
> If the act, occurrence, or use does not adversely affect the physical condition of or title to the property, then it is not a material fact. Therefore the fact or suspicion that the property or neighboring property is or was the site of a murder, suicide, or other death; rape or other sex crime; assault or other violent crime; robbery or burglary; illegal drug activity; gang-related activity; or political or religious activity is not a material fact and need not be disclosed *[RCW 18.86.010(9)]*.

However, unless otherwise agreed, the licensee has no duty to:

- conduct an independent inspection of:
  - the property
  - either party's financial condition
- independently verify the accuracy or completeness of any statement made by either party or by any source reasonably believed by the licensee to be reliable

Duties of Licensees to All Parties						
Reasonable Skill & Care	Honesty & Good Faith	Present All Offers	Disclose Material Facts	Accounting	Pamphlet	Agency Disclosure

When acting as an agent, a licensee has additional duties that include the following:

- be loyal to the principal by taking no adverse or detrimental action to the principal's interest in a transaction
- timely disclose to the principal any conflicts of interest
- advise the principal to get expert advice on matters beyond the agent's expertise
- not disclose any confidential information from or about the principal, except under subpoena or court order, even after termination of the agency relationship

> **Confidential information** is information from or concerning a principal or a licensee that:
> - was acquired by the licensee during the course of an agency relationship with the principal
> - the principal reasonably expects to be kept confidential
> - the principal has not disclosed or authorized to be disclosed to third parties
> - would, if disclosed, operate to the detriment of the principal
> - the principal would not be obligated to personally disclose to the other party
>
> [RCW 18.86.010(7)]

In addition to these duties, an agent has a duty to make a good faith and continuous effort to find a buyer for a property and find a property for the buyer. This is the only duty that may be waived.

Duties of an Agent to a Principal				
Loyalty	Disclose Conflicts	Advise Expert Advice	Confidentiality	Good Faith Effort

SELLER'S AGENT AND BUYER'S AGENT [RCW 18.86.040, -.050]

Unless otherwise agreed to in writing, after providing the required pamphlet on the law of real estate agency, the seller's agent must make a good faith and continuous effort to find a buyer for the property until a contract of sale is created. While a seller's agent must present any written offer received after such a contract is created, he/she is not obligated to continue to seek additional offers to purchase the property once the property is subject to an existing contract for sale.

A seller's agent may show alternative properties not owned by the seller to prospective buyers and may list competing properties for sale without breaching any duty to the seller, unless otherwise agreed to in writing.

For Example

Prospective buyer Bianca attends an open house and indicates she is not interested in purchasing that property. Listing agent Lori would be able to show Bianca other properties without breaching the duty of loyalty to the seller. However, if the seller accepts an offer from Bianca, and Bianca indicates she wants to continue looking at other properties, Lori should not show other properties to Bianca. While such activity could help Bianca to realize that the transaction is advantageous to her and should be closed, it could just as likely be adverse or detrimental to the seller's interest in the transaction.

For a buyer's agent this duty means that, unless otherwise agreed to in writing, after the agent has provided the agency pamphlet, he/she must make a good faith and continuous effort to find a property for the buyer. However, a buyer's agent is not obligated to:

- seek additional properties to purchase while the buyer is a party to an existing contract to purchase
- show properties for which there is no written agreement to pay compensation to the buyer's agent

A buyer's agent may show properties in which the buyer is interested to other prospective buyers without breaching any duty to the buyer.

An agent's duties are limited to those specified, unless additional duties are agreed to in writing and signed by the agent. Parties may enter into written agreements that impose greater responsibilities on a licensee than these limited agent provisions require. For example, a client may enter into a long-term relationship with a licensee or give the licensee greater responsibilities in concluding a transaction. If the licensee does negotiate such an agreement, then he/she is no longer considered a limited agent. The customary common-law fiduciary obligations of an agent to a principal apply in that circumstance.

DUAL AGENCY [RCW 18.86.060]

Under the Brokerage Relationships Act, a licensee may act as a dual agent only under the following circumstances:

- with the written consent of both parties to the transaction, which must include a statement of the terms of compensation
- after the agent has provided both parties with a pamphlet explaining agency law

Therefore, to have the protection of the law, the dual agency must be disclosed the dual agent must:

- take no action that is adverse or detrimental to either party's interest in a transaction
- timely disclose to both parties any conflicts of interest
- advise both parties to get expert advice on matters beyond the dual agent's expertise
- not disclose any confidential information from or about either party, except under subpoena or court order, even after termination of the agency relationship
- make a good faith and continuous effort to find a buyer for the property until there is a sale contract for the property
- make a good faith and continuous effort, for which he/she would be compensated, to find a property for the buyer until the buyer is a party to a purchase agreement

A dual agent may show alternative properties, not owned by the seller, to prospective buyers and may list competing properties for sale without breaching any duty to the seller. An agent may show properties in which the buyer is interested to other prospective buyers without breaching any duty to the buyer.

AGENCY TERMS [RCW 18.86.070, -.080]

An agency relationship starts when a licensee begins to provide brokerage services and continues until:

- he/she completes performance
- the agreement expires
- the parties mutually agree to terminate the relationship
- termination by notice from either party to the other, although termination does not affect the contractual rights of either party

Except as otherwise agreed to in writing, a licensee owes no further duty after termination of the agency relationship, other than to:

- account for money and property received during the relationship
- avoid disclosing confidential information

A broker may be paid by anyone. An agreement to pay compensation or the payment of compensation does not establish an agency relationship between the party who paid the compensation and the licensee.

A seller or buyer may allow a seller's or buyer's agent to share with another broker the compensation paid by the principal. A broker may be paid by more than one party if the parties consent in writing at or before signing an offer. A buyer's agent or dual agent may be paid based on the purchase price without breaching any duty to the buyer. Neither the buyer nor the seller need pay a licensee unless they enter into a written agreement with the licensee specifying the terms of compensation.

LIABILITY [RCW 18.86.090, -.100]

A principal does not have vicarious liability for acts, errors, or omissions performed by his/her agent or subagent, unless the principal:

- participated in or authorized them
- benefited from them, and a court determines it is highly probable that the claimant would be unable to enforce a judgment against the agent or subagent

A licensee has no vicarious liability for acts, errors, or omissions of subagents, unless he/she participated in or authorized them. However, a firm is liable for acts, errors, or omissions by a broker licensed to the firm.

Unless otherwise agreed to in writing, a principal does not have imputed knowledge of any facts known by his/her agent or subagent, and a licensee does not have imputed knowledge of any facts known by a subagent. However, a designated broker or managing broker does have imputed knowledge of facts known by the brokers under his/her supervision.

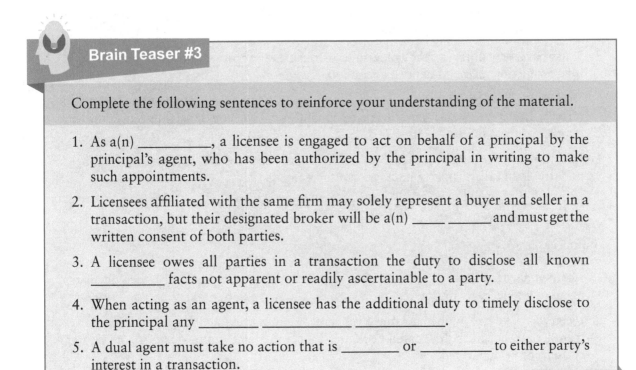

Brain Teaser #3

Complete the following sentences to reinforce your understanding of the material.

1. As a(n) _____, a licensee is engaged to act on behalf of a principal by the principal's agent, who has been authorized by the principal in writing to make such appointments.

2. Licensees affiliated with the same firm may solely represent a buyer and seller in a transaction, but their designated broker will be a(n) _____ and must get the written consent of both parties.

3. A licensee owes all parties in a transaction the duty to disclose all known _____ facts not apparent or readily ascertainable to a party.

4. When acting as an agent, a licensee has the additional duty to timely disclose to the principal any _____ _____ _____.

5. A dual agent must take no action that is _____ or _____ to either party's interest in a transaction.

Brain Teaser Answers

Brain Teaser #1

1. A licensee is required to disclose his/her **license** status in any form of advertising utilized.
2. When negotiating a sales agreement, the licensee must present all **written** offers to the seller.
3. A license will be **immediately** suspended if the Department of Social and Health Services certifies that the licensee is not in compliance with a support order.
4. A licensee cannot require as a condition of providing real estate services that a consumer obtain title insurance from a title insurance agent in which the licensee has a **financial** interest.
5. Each designated broker must establish a written office policy that includes a procedure for referring **home inspectors** to buyers or sellers.

Brain Teaser #2

1. The **designated** broker is responsible for deposits, disbursements, or transfers of clients' funds received and held in trust.
2. Trust bank accounts for real estate sales or business opportunity transactions must be interest-bearing **demand** deposit accounts.
3. Except for property management trust accounts, the firm must maintain a pooled interest-bearing demand deposit trust account as a Housing Trust Fund account for deposit of trust funds of $**10,000** or less.
4. Each owner of property managed by the firm must be provided a **summary** statement as provided in the property management agreement.
5. Property management commissions must be withdrawn from the trust account at least once **monthly**.

Brain Teaser #3

1. As a **subagent**, a licensee is engaged to act on behalf of a principal by the principal's agent, who has been authorized by the principal in writing to make such appointments.
2. Licensees affiliated with the same firm may solely represent a buyer and seller in a transaction, but their designated broker will be a **dual agent** and must get the written consent of both parties.
3. A licensee owes all parties in a transaction the duty to disclose all known **material** facts not apparent or readily ascertainable to a party.
4. When acting as an agent, a licensee has the additional duty to timely disclose to the principal any **conflicts of interest**.
5. A dual agent must take no action that is **adverse** or **detrimental** to either party's interest in a transaction.

Review — Real Estate License Law and Regulations III

This lesson explains the professional responsibilities related to activities involving licensees in real estate transactions. This includes property management and the handling of clients' trust funds. Agency disclosure requirements and duties are also reviewed.

A licensee is required to disclose his/her license status in any form of advertising utilized.

All advertising or solicitations for brokerage services must include the firm's name or an assumed name as licensed, except for ads for personally owned property. A licensee is prohibited from making, printing, publishing, or distributing false statements, descriptions, or promises that would reasonably induce a person to act, if the licensee knew or could reasonably have known of their falsity.

Licensees must deliver (or have delivered) each purchase and sale agreement, listing agreement, and any other similar instrument to all parties signing them within a reasonable time after signing.

Whether buying, selling, or leasing an interest in real property directly or through a third party, a licensee must disclose in writing that he/she holds a real estate license. A licensee must also make certain disclosures in a transaction, including providing a pamphlet on the law of real estate agency to all parties to whom he/she renders real estate brokerage services and before the parties perform certain actions; disclosing in writing to all parties to whom he/she renders brokerage services, and before any party signs an offer, which party he represents; disclosing to all parties in the transaction whether he/she will charge or accept compensation from more than one party in the transaction; disclosing any commission, rebate, or direct profit he/she will accept or charge on expenditures made for his/her principal; and more.

A real estate agent has a duty to advise his/her client (i.e., the seller, the buyer, or both the seller and the buyer if he/she is a dual agent) to seek expert advice on matters relating to the transaction that are beyond the agent's expertise.

Grounds for the suspension or revocation of a real estate license include engaging in conduct that demonstrates bad faith, dishonesty, untrustworthiness, or incompetence; failing to perform all acts required by a real estate agreement as quickly as possible; making material false statements; and knowingly committing any material fraud, misrepresentation, scheme, or device when any other person lawfully relies upon the licensee's conduct.

A licensee cannot, because of a person's race, color, creed, sex, age, national origin, marital status, familial status, military status, sexual orientation, or disability discriminate against that person in any aspect of a real estate transaction.

No part of a commission for brokerage services or other compensation can be paid by a licensed firm or broker to any person who performs real estate brokerage services and is not properly licensed; by a licensed firm to a broker not licensed with the firm; or by a licensed broker to any person, whether licensed or not, except through the firm's designated broker.

A designated broker is responsible for the administration of trust funds and accounts. He/She must ensure that his/her affiliated licensees safeguard funds or advance fees received from any principal or any party to a real estate or business opportunity transaction, property management agreement, contract, or mortgage collection agreement by holding them in trust for the purposes of the transaction or agreement.

All licensees must keep their own funds physically separated from all moneys collected for clients and being held for disbursement for or to clients. The licensee cannot commingle (i.e., mix) funds of clients or customers with his/her own funds or convert any money, contract, deed, note, mortgage, or other evidence of title delivered to him/her in trust or on condition. This means he/she cannot use these funds for his/her own benefit or for the benefit of any person not entitled to it.

All real estate transaction funds over which the firm will exercise control must be deposited in one or more separate bank accounts designated as real estate trust fund accounts, in a Washington state banking institution insured by the Federal Deposit Insurance Corporation (FDIC), or in the share insurance fund of the National Credit Union Administration (NCUA).

Except for property management trust accounts, the firm must maintain a pooled interest-bearing demand deposit trust account as a Housing Trust Fund account for deposit of trust funds of $10,000 or less.

Funds cannot be disbursed from a trust account to pay bank charges, other than those that may be deducted from interest-bearing accounts; to pay for business overhead expenses of the real estate firm; for items not pertaining to a specific real estate transaction; in excess of the actual amount held in the trust account for that specific purpose; in advance of the closing of a real estate or business opportunity transaction; or before the occurrence of a condition set forth in a purchase and sale agreement without a written release from both the purchaser and seller.

A designated broker is responsible for ensuring trust accounts are properly administered, including properly setting up and reconciling a trust account; depositing, holding, disbursing, receipting, posting, and recording funds; accounting to principals; and notifying principals and cooperating licensees of material facts.

For each property managed, a firm must have, and retain for three years following its termination, a written management agreement signed by the owner and designated broker. A designated broker who manages properties must comply with all rules pertaining to trust accounts, except that funds for property management transactions need not be placed in a pooled interest-bearing account.

Whether a licensee is an agent or a nonagent, he/she owes all parties in a transaction the duty to exercise reasonable skill and care; deal honestly and in good faith; account in a timely manner for all money and property received; present all written offers and other written communications in a timely manner; provide a pamphlet on the law of real estate agency to any party to whom he/she renders services before the occurrence of certain events; before a party signs an offer, disclose whether he/she represents the buyer, the seller, both parties, or neither; and disclose all known material facts not apparent or readily ascertainable to a party.

When acting as an agent, a licensee has the additional duties to be loyal to the principal by taking no action adverse or detrimental to the principal's interest in a transaction; timely disclose to the principal any conflicts of interest; advise the principal to get expert advice on matters beyond the agent's expertise; and not disclose any confidential information from or about the principal, except under subpoena or court order, even after termination of the agency relationship.

Unless otherwise agreed to in writing, after providing the required pamphlet on the law of real estate agency, the seller's agent must make a good faith and continuous effort to find a buyer for the property until a contract of sale is created. A buyer's agent must make a good faith and continuous effort to find a property for the buyer. A licensee may act as a dual agent only with the written consent of both parties to the transaction, which must include a statement of the terms of compensation, and after the agent has provided both parties with a pamphlet explaining agency law.

An agency relationship starts when a licensee begins to provide brokerage services and continues until he/she completes performance; the agreement expires; the parties mutually agree to terminate the relationship; or termination by notice from either party to the other, although termination does not affect the contractual rights of either party.

A broker may be paid by anyone. An agreement to pay compensation or the payment of compensation does not establish an agency relationship between the party who paid the compensation and the licensee.

A principal does not have vicarious liability for acts, errors, or omissions performed by his/her agent or subagent, unless the principal participated, authorized the agent or subagent, or benefited from him/her, and a court determines it is highly probable that the claimant would be unable to enforce a judgment against the agent or subagent.

This concludes the review for Real Estate License Law and Regulations III.

Washington Laws

CHAPTER 4

OVERVIEW

This lesson reviews some specific state laws related to real property transactions. The lesson begins with water rights and community property, and then it continues with taxes, construction liens, and foreclosures. This is followed by a discussion of the Residential Landlord-Tenant Act and leases. State laws addressing discrimination and escrow conclude the lesson.

Upon completion of this chapter, the student should be able to:

1. define and describe water rights and community property
2. describe the provisions of homestead laws
3. detail the manner by which a governmental body determines and assesses the amount of taxes
4. identify the procedures for enforcing tax liens
5. explain real property excise tax requirements and identify affected real property transactions
6. describe and give examples of mechanics' liens and materialmen's liens
7. explain what happens in a foreclosure action or a forfeiture action
8. outline the elements of a seller disclosure statement
9. describe the elements of the Residential Landlord-Tenant Act
10. discuss the basic provisions in a residential lease
11. demonstrate familiarity with the relevant Washington state statutes against discrimination
12. identify local and state agencies responsible for the enforcement of the fair housing laws
13. describe who is authorized to perform closing services under the Escrow Agent Registration Act

Water Rights

Washington, like most western states, is an appropriation doctrine state and not a riparian rights state. State statute provides that water in Washington is considered to be owned by the general public. Therefore, a **riparian owner** (i.e., one who owns land along the bank of a river or stream) does not automatically have the right to use water. Instead, the state grants, or appropriates, rights to use water to riparian and nonriparian owners (e.g., the state may give permission to a nonriparian owner of a farm to use water from a nearby lake).

To be allowed to divert waters for private use, a landowner must obtain a water rights certificate from the Supervisor of Water Resources at the Department of Ecology. The certificate shows the following:

- the period during which the right may be exercised
- the point of diversion
- the place of use
- the maximum quantity of water that may be diverted
- the land to which the water right is appurtenant

The date on which the application for the certificate is filed establishes who has the first right to use available water during the times when there is not enough water to satisfy the needs of all the water right holders in an area.

Community Property
[RCW 26.16]

Under state law, all real property in Washington and all personal property anywhere acquired by a husband and wife during a valid marriage or by persons in a state-registered domestic partnership is **community property** unless specifically acquired by one or the other as separate property.

Separate property is property that is owned and may be conveyed individually by a husband, wife, or domestic partner. It includes:

- property owned before the marriage or partnership
- rents and profits from separate property
- property acquired with the proceeds of separate property
- property acquired during marriage or partnership by devise, inheritance, or gift

However, separate property may be converted to community property by:

- commingling it with community property
- use of a **community property agreement**, making all property currently owned or later acquired by either spouse or partner community property, regardless of how or when it was acquired, and providing for all community property to automatically pass to a surviving spouse or partner

Either spouse or partner may manage and control community property without the consent of the other if acting alone, but neither can:

- encumber or sell community household goods, furnishings, or appliances unless the other also signs the legal instrument encumbering or conveying title to the property
- give away community property without the express or implied consent of the other
- sell, convey, or encumber the community real property alone

Therefore to be valid, contracts for these purposes require the signatures of both spouses or partners, and a single person or surviving spouse or partner must indicate on a deed, contract, or mortgage his/her marital status to establish for the record that there is no community property interest being conveyed.

Although either spouse or partner may convey ownership of separate property without the other's signature on the deed, a title company may request the other either to sign a quitclaim deed releasing any possible interest in the property or to co-sign all the transaction documents (e.g., the listing agreement, the sales agreement, the deed, etc). Thus, many deeds may indicate that the conveyance is for the grantor's separate property but still contain the acknowledged signature of the grantor's spouse or partner.

If there is no community property agreement, a spouse or partner may bequeath separate property and a one-half interest in the community property to anyone. If a spouse or partner dies **intestate** (i.e., without leaving a valid will), then the following will take place:

- all community property vests in the surviving spouse or partner
- the decedent's separate property is divided between the surviving spouse or partner and the decedent's children, with each party inheriting 50% of it

Homestead Exemption
[RCW 6.13]

A homestead exemption may protect a homeowner from foreclosure on **unsecured liens** (i.e., judgments and other liens in which the property was not originally offered as security for the debt). It will not defeat foreclosure on secured liens, such as mortgages, deeds of trust, or homeowners or condominium association liens.

The exemption is provided only for a person's **homestead** (i.e., the real or personal property actually intended or used as his/her principal home). This includes the dwelling house or mobile home in which the owner resides or intends to reside, with appurtenant buildings and the land on which he/she is situated, as well as improved or unimproved land on which the owner intends to place a house or mobile home in which he/she will reside.

The exemption releases the residence from attachment and from execution or forced sale for the debts of the owner up to a limit of the lesser of:

- the net value of the homestead (i.e., the market value less all senior liens and encumbrances)
- $125,000 for land, mobile home, and improvements, or $15,000 for other personal property

A homestead is created automatically as of the time the owner occupies the property as his/her principal residence. It may be terminated by the filing of a declaration of abandonment or by presumption of abandonment. It is presumed abandoned if the owner vacates the property for at least six consecutive months.

When homestead property is sold in order to acquire a new homestead, the exemption protects the sale proceeds and the new property for one year, and the purchaser of the sold homestead is not liable for the seller's judgment.

Taxes

PROPERTY TAX

In Washington, the tax assessor determines what real and personal property is taxable, assesses the property, and gets it listed on the tax rolls. The preliminary work must begin each year by December 1 and end by May 31. In assessing the property, the assessor must determine its true value and its fair value as of January 1, the assessment date. The assessed value is supposed to be 100% of the true and fair value.

In the assessment of real property, the market data approach is most widely used. When the market data approach is not appropriate, the cost or income approaches may be used. Land is assessed based on its current use, rather than its highest and best use, if it is classified as:

- open space land
- farm and agricultural land
- timberland or forestland

If such uses are changed or a new owner does not file a notice of compliance with the assessor, then there may be a seven-year or 10-year rollback of the taxes, plus in some cases, interest and penalties.

Property taxes become a lien on real property on the first day of the tax year, January 1. They remain a lien until paid. When real property is sold and there is no agreement as to who will pay the taxes, the buyer and seller are each liable for a prorated amount.

For Example

The annual tax is $1,095. The first half of the year's taxes has been paid.

The closing date is June 1. The seller's share of the taxes is for January through May. Adding the days in each month, this totals 151 days. The buyer's share is for 30 days.

Because the annual tax is $1,095, the daily tax is $3 ($1,095 ÷ 365). Because the seller paid up to July 1 (30 days beyond the closing date), the seller will be credited with $90 ($3 × 30). The buyer will be debited for this amount.

If the taxes for the entire year are to be paid at closing, the seller will still be reimbursed and credited his $90, but the buyer will be debited the $90 and the $547.50 due for the second half of the year, for a total of $637.50.

The county treasurer mails out tax statements to each taxpayer in the county by February 14. Taxes may be paid beginning February 15. They are not due, however, until April 30. Taxes may be paid in two installments:

- half by April 30
- the other half by October 31

If the first half is not paid by April 30, the entire year's tax is delinquent as of May 1 and a penalty is assessed at:

- 1% interest per month from May 1 until paid
- if still unpaid as of May 31, an additional 3%
- if still unpaid as of November 30, an additional 8%

Thus, after 12 months of delinquency, there would be 23% interest and a penalty owed (i.e., 12% + 3% + 8%).

If the first tax installment is paid on time or is paid with any interest and penalty due before October 31, then the second installment will be due October 31. If this tax payment is not paid, then it becomes delinquent as of November 1. A 1% penalty per month would begin to be charged on the overdue half at that time, and the 8% additional penalty would be levied on the overdue half as of November 30.

EXCISE TAX [RCW 82.45]

An **excise tax** of 1.28% of the sales price (plus an additional amount added by local authorities) is imposed on the transfer of the title to, or of an estate in, real property when valuable consideration is given. The tax does not apply to transfers:

- by gift, devise, inheritance, or property settlement under divorce proceedings
- of leasehold interests
- by deed in lieu of foreclosure
- by loan assumption where no other valuable consideration is given

The tax is a specific lien on the property, from the time it is sold until the tax is paid. The seller is liable for this payment. If the tax is not paid, then the property may be foreclosed or the seller may be sued for a personal judgment. There is an interest penalty of 1% if the tax is not paid within 30 days of the date of sale. Additional penalties are added 60 days and 90 days after the sale.

When the County Treasurer receives the tax, he/she will:

- stamp the document
- complete a real estate excise tax affidavit
- issue a receipt showing the tax has been paid

A document conveying an interest cannot be accepted by the County Auditor for recording until the tax has been paid and the Treasurer's stamp has been affixed to it or the Treasurer has noted that tax is not due.

Construction Liens
[RCW 60.04]

Mechanics' liens and materialmen's liens are considered statutory liens, as state statute gives people who have furnished work or material (i.e., **materialmen**) for the improvement of real property the right to place a lien on that property if they are not paid. A claim of lien must be filed within 90 days after the work has ceased or materials have been delivered. Once recorded, the lien's effective date is the day the work started.

The claimant has eight months to file a suit for foreclosure if he/she is not paid. If he/she does not file for foreclosure within that time, the property will no longer be security for the debt and cannot be foreclosed upon. However, the claimant can file for an unsecured judgment against the property owner.

Foreclosure and Forfeiture
(RCW 61.12, 61.21, 61.24)

If a mortgagor defaults on the promises he/she makes in the note or mortgage, the lender has the right to sue on the note to obtain a judgment or request that the property be **foreclosed** and sold through court auction in the superior court of the county in which the land is located. **Foreclosure** is the lender's remedy when a buyer borrows money to purchase real estate and then defaults in repayment. The real estate is **collateral** for the loan, so if there is a **default**, the lender has the legal right to force the property to be sold to pay off the loan.

There are three different types of financing structures that can be used in Washington. What they all have in common is that they combine two elements:

- First, the borrower **promises to pay** back the amount of the loan, with interest.
- Second, the borrower grants the lender a **security interest** in the property, which creates a **consensual lien** and makes the property collateral for the loan.

The three different ways to structure financing are:

- **promissory note**, secured by a **mortgage**
- promissory note, secured by a **deed of trust**
- **real estate contract**

PROMISSORY NOTE

A valid promissory note signed by the borrower and given to the lender provides legally acceptable evidence of the borrower's debt and his/her promise to repay the debt. It establishes:

- who is the borrower
- who is the lender
- the amount of the debt
- the interest rate (if the rate is adjustable, it explains when and how it adjusts)
- the terms of repayment

The note should always state that the debt is secured by real property, identifying the security instrument by date or recording number.

If a borrower defaults in payment, then the lender can sue to collect on the note. However, this is usually not done in the context of a real estate loan because presumably the reason the borrower stopped paying is because they don't have resources. Instead, lenders typically foreclose on their security interest in the collateral property, forcing it to be sold and using the sale proceeds to pay off the loan. **The process depends on the security instrument used.**

MORTGAGE

In common usage, the word "mortgage" is used to reference any loan secured by real estate. However, technically a mortgage isn't a loan, it is a type of **security instrument** used to secure such a loan. The loan terms are in the promissory note; the mortgage is **recorded** and this is what attaches to the title of the property, creating the lien that secures the debt.

Prior to 1965, a mortgage was the only way to secure a promissory note, because at that time there was no **deed of trust**.

Mortgages, which usually do not contain a power of sale clause, are usually foreclosed through a **judicial foreclosure**, which means filing a civil lawsuit and going to court. Judicial foreclosure is slow, expensive, and cumbersome. Lenders prefer to avoid it except in unusual circumstances.

If the lender prevails, then the judge will order a decree of foreclosure, which causes the property to be sold at auction by the sheriff of the county in which the property is located.

Sale proceeds go first to pay the expenses of the sale, and then to any delinquent taxes or tax liens, and finally to the lender. If the sale proceeds are less than the amount owed to the lender, then the lender can get a **deficiency judgment** for the shortfall.

However, there is a **right of redemption**, meaning that for up to 12 months after the sale, depending on circumstances, the borrower has the right to cure the default and get title back. **The successful bidder at the auction does not get a deed immediately.** They receive a "**certificate of sale.**" They only get a deed from the sheriff later, after the redemption period has expired. This redemption period is one year and is either:

- shortened to eight months if the:
  - lender waives his/her right to a deficiency judgment
  - mortgage states the property is not used primarily for agricultural purposes

- eliminated entirely, in which case the purchaser gets a deed immediately, if the property:
  - is nonagricultural
  - is improved with a structure
  - has been abandoned for six months or more

Foreclosure wipes out all junior liens and encumbrances.

DEED OF TRUST

In 1965, the legislature created a new type of security instrument by statute. **The Deed of Trust Act** is set forth in RCW **61.24**.

There are three parties in a deed of trust (DOT). At closing the deed gets recorded first, transferring title from the seller to the buyer. The DOT is recorded immediately after that.

The **grantors** (**trustors**) are the borrowers. The DOT transfers title to the property to the **trustee**, which is usually a title insurance company. This is not considered a true legal title, but rather a power of sale for the trustee to sell the property at foreclosure without court approval if there is a default in the payment of the promissory note referenced in the DOT. The DOT instructs the trustee to hold title to the property in trust for the protection of the **beneficiary**, which is the lender. In the event of a default, the beneficiary can give written notice to the trustee to initiate the **nonjudicial foreclosure** process.

The first step is a **Notice of Default**. This is not recorded, so it is not public record. It gives formal notice to the borrower and others that have a recorded interest in the property that they are in default and have **30 days to cure**. If the default is not timely cured, then the trustee issues a **Notice of Trustee's Sale**. This document is recorded and gives constructive notice (public notice) that a foreclosure sale will occur on a date that must be at least **90 days** after the recording of the notice.

The sale can be **continued** (delayed) if the borrower contacts the lender and asks for time to list the property for sale or tries to negotiate a modification of the loan. To stop the sale, the grantor would then have to redeem the property by paying off the total principal balance, plus interest and costs, or succeed in legal action in superior court to have the sale stopped. The borrower can cure the defaults and **reinstate the loan** up to **11 days** before the sale. If he/she does so, then the sale is canceled and the loan remains in place.

If the sale proceeds, then the lender (beneficiary) can **credit bid** up to the amount they are owed, and if nobody bids higher, the lender will get title to the property. The lender will then usually list it for sale with a broker and use the sale proceeds to pay off the loan.

If somebody outbids the lender, then the property goes to the highest bidder. The winner must pay in the form of cash, certified check, cashier's check, money order, or verified electronic transfer immediately, and receives on the spot a **Trustee's Deed** that conveys title. The winner is entitled to possession of the property on the 20th day after the sale.

It is important to note that foreclosure of the DOT wipes out all junior liens or encumbrances. **There is no deficiency judgment in a non-judicial**

foreclosure. This is the fundamental "bargain" of the DOT Act. Lenders get a faster, less expensive, and easier way to foreclose, but in exchange they give up the right to a deficiency judgment. BUT, there is also **no right of redemption after the sale**. Winning bidder gets title immediately, and the foreclosed grantor (borrower) cannot get it back even a day later. The money received at the sale is used to pay off:

- the expenses of the sale
- the deed of trust
- any other liens against the property, such as taxes, in order of priority

If there is still a surplus, then it is given to the foreclosed grantor.

REAL ESTATE CONTRACT

The real estate contract is an entirely different form of financing. It encumbers the seller's title and is a cloud on the title until the seller does one of the following:

- delivers a deed to the buyer
- receives a quitclaim deed from the buyer releasing the buyer's interest
- takes legal action to remove the buyer's interest from the title

The real estate contract replaces both the promissory note and the security instrument (mortgage or deed of trust). It gets recorded against title at closing. The real estate contract is commonly used in eastern Washington because a DOT cannot be used on agricultural property. It is often faster and easier to enforce a real estate contract than to judicially foreclose a mortgage.

The buyer does not get legal title immediately after a real estate contract is drawn; he/she has equitable title in the property only while the seller continues to hold legal title until the contract has been fully paid. The buyer gets legal title via a **fulfillment deed**, which is recorded at the end of the contract after it has been fully paid.

If the buyer defaults on the contract, then the seller may do any of the following:

- sue for any delinquent payment
- accelerate the balance due and sue for payment of the balance
- sue for specific performance
- forfeit the buyer's interest

If there is a default, then the seller may record a **notice of intent to forfeit**, which states that if defaults are not cured within **90 days**, the seller intends to exercise its power of **forfeiture**. If defaults are not cured within that time, then the seller then records a **declaration of forfeiture**, which is the formal step that cancels the contract and restores title to the seller. **The seller gets to keep all amounts paid prior to forfeiture, and the buyer loses everything.**

Because of the declaration of forfeiture, the buyer's rights, title, and interest in the property are terminated, as well as the buyer's rights under the contract. Ownership of all sums paid under the contract and all improvements made to the property, as well as unharvested crops on the property, are granted to the seller 10 days after the forfeiture.

To protect buyers from this harsh result, Washington adopted special rules in 1986 that allow buyers to file lawsuits seeking to **enjoin the forfeiture**. They can also **petition for a judicial sale**, but only if the fair market value of the property "substantially exceeds the unpaid and unperformed obligations secured by the contract" (according to Title 61 of the Washington State Legislature). The sale is like a Sheriff's sale of a mortgage but without any redemption period or deficiency judgment. This means if there is a substantial amount of equity in the property the seller will get only what is owed on the remaining term of the contract and the buyer will get the rest.

Seller's Disclosure
[RCW 64.06]

A seller of commercial real estate or improved or unimproved residential real estate in Washington is required to give the buyer a complete seller disclosure statement, unless one of the following takes place:

- buyer waives the right to receive the disclosure statement
- transfer is exempt from the requirement

The form of the disclosure statements, which is set forth in the state statutes, requires disclosure of matters related to the title and the condition of the property based upon the seller's personal knowledge.

For each disclosure item, the seller answers either "No," "Yes," "Don't know," or "NA" (Not Applicable). If he/she answers "Yes" to a question, in most instances he/she will need to provide an explanation or a copy of the document referred to.

The disclosure statements are not disclosures from a real estate licensee or a warranty by the seller or any real estate licensee involved in the transaction.

Unless the buyer waives the right to receive the disclosure statement, the seller must give the buyer a completed, signed, and dated disclosure statement within five business days of acceptance of an offer to purchase, unless otherwise agreed.

If the answer to any of the questions in the section entitled "Environmental" is "Yes," then the buyer may not waive the receipt of the Environmental section of the seller disclosure statement.

Within three business days from receipt of the statement (or as otherwise agreed), the buyer may either:

- approve and accept the statement
- give written notice of rescission of the sales agreement

If after completing the statement the seller becomes aware of additional information or an adverse change occurs that makes any of the disclosures inaccurate, then the seller must either:

- amend the disclosure statement and deliver the amendment to the buyer
- at least three days prior to the closing date, take whatever corrective action is necessary to restore the accuracy of the disclosure

Recent Washington court cases indicate the courts are currently in flux as to the level of reliance buyers can place on seller disclosures in determining structural defects and other issues that could affect the condition of property they are interested in purchasing. The Washington Department of Licensing is recommending that real estate licensees advise buyers to conduct or have done thorough inspections prior to purchasing any property instead of using seller disclosures as their primary determining factor.

Residential Landlords and Tenants [RCW 59.18]

RESIDENTIAL LANDLORD-TENANT ACT

The Residential Landlord-Tenant Act (the Act) applies to rentals of residences in homes, multiplexes, apartments, and mobile homes. The Act:

- establishes minimum habitability standards and procedures for correcting housing defects
- institutes notice procedures
- prohibits unfair reprisals, lockouts, and **distress** (i.e., taking the tenant's property until the rent is paid) for rent
- establishes procedures for arbitration of disputes
- establishes requirements for trust accounts for damage deposits
- establishes specific time periods for refund of deposits or notice of reasons for nonrefund of deposits
- governs the landlord's right of entry
- protects a tenant against retaliation by the landlord

Landlord Obligations

The landlord must keep the property fit for human habitation, including:

- maintaining the premises to comply with all state and local statutes and codes that affect the tenant's health and safety
- maintaining all structural components
- keeping common and shared areas clean and safe
- providing for control of insects, rodents, and other pests, except when caused by tenant (in single-family residences, the landlord does not have to control infestations that occur during tenancy)
- providing the tenant with adequate locks and keys
- maintaining all electrical, plumbing, heating, and other facilities he/she supplies

- maintaining the dwelling in a weather-tight condition
- providing garbage cans and arrange for waste removal (except for single-family residences)
- providing adequate heat, water, and hot water
- providing the name and address of the landlord by statement, in the rental agreement, or by notice clearly posted on the premises
- notifying the tenant immediately of any change of landlord personally, by certified mail, or updated posting
- naming an agent who resides in the county where the premises are located if the landlord lives out of state
- providing written information about fire safety and mold
- providing smoke and carbon monoxide detectors and ensuring they work properly when a new tenant moves in
- providing a receipt for fees or deposits charged to hold a dwelling and giving a written description of the conditions under which the deposit may be returned
- providing a receipt for any cash payment or, upon request, any other payment made by the tenant

If a landlord fails to carry out any duties required by law, then the tenant may deliver written notice. If the tenant gives proper notice, then the landlord must begin work on the defective condition as soon as possible.

If the landlord fails to carry out his/her responsibilities after receipt of proper notice, the tenant can:

- move out without the normal 20-day notice
- sue to have the rent reduced
- go to an arbitrator
- contract with a third party to have the deficiency corrected at the landlord's expense
- correct the condition himself

Nonrefundable Fees

Restrictions are imposed on fees a landlord may charge a prospective tenant. If the landlord takes a nonrefundable fee, then there must be a written rental agreement that specifies the fee as being nonrefundable.

Deposits

Deposits must be kept in a trust account in a bank, savings and loan association, mutual savings bank, or licensed escrow account located in Washington. The tenant must be given a written receipt for the deposit.

Within 14 days after termination of the rental agreement and vacation of the premises, the landlord must deliver personally or by first-class mail to the tenant's last known address:

- a full and specific statement of the basis for retaining any of the deposit
- the payment of any refund due to the tenant

Tenant Obligations

The Act also spells out the obligations of the tenant and provides remedies for landlords of tenants who do not meet those obligations.

A tenant cannot unreasonably withhold consent to the landlord to enter his/her rental unit for any of the following actions:

- inspect the premises
- make necessary repairs
- exhibit the unit to prospective purchasers or tenants

The tenant must:

- comply with all laws
- keep the premises clean
- properly dispose of rubbish
- properly use fixtures and appliances
- not damage any part of the dwelling
- not permit a nuisance
- not engage in drug-related activity
- maintain the smoke and carbon monoxide detection devices
- not unreasonably withhold consent for the landlord to enter the dwelling to inspect, repair, or show the unit
- pay rent

Defaults and Evictions

If the tenant defaults, then the landlord has remedies available, including correcting the problem himself/herself if it is correctable or having the tenant evicted.

A tenant cannot be physically removed from the premises for any reason until the following process is complete:

1. if the tenant refuses to move after the tenancy has been terminated, then the landlord may bring a lawsuit (i.e., unlawful detainer action) to evict the tenant
2. the tenant must appear in court to protect his rights; if the court rules in favor of the landlord, then the sheriff will be instructed to move the tenant out if he/she does not leave voluntarily
3. the tenant may be required to pay the landlord's damages and attorney fees

Lockouts, turning off utilities, seizing a tenant's property, etc., are illegal.

LEASE PROVISIONS

The basic provisions of a residential lease include:

- the term and provisions for termination and renewal of the lease
- with regard to rent:
  - the amount
  - when and where it is payable
  - when a late fee will be imposed and for what amount
- the amount of security deposit and the terms under which it is refundable

- the purpose and amount of any nonrefundable fees
- tenant responsibilities regarding use and maintenance of the premises
- landlord responsibilities regarding provision of habitable premises
- policies regarding pets, smoking, parking, etc.
- the landlord's right to access to the premises

Fair Housing Issues

When offering real estate for sale or rent, a real estate agent must be aware of state, local, and federal laws pertaining to discrimination.

In Washington, the Real Estate Brokers and Managing Brokers Act [RCW 18.85] prohibits licensees from discriminating against persons in hiring or sales activity and from violating any of the provisions of local, county, state, or federal anti-discrimination law.

Furthermore, Washington's law against discrimination [RCW 49.60] prohibits practices of discrimination by any person in a real estate transaction (i.e., the sale, appraisal, brokering, exchange, purchase, rental, or lease of real property; the transaction or application for a real estate loan; or the provision of brokerage services).

This law is enforced by the Washington State Human Rights Commission and has enforcement provisions and penalties similar to those established under the federal Fair Housing Act. It has fewer exemptions than federal law (e.g., it applies to all types of real estate, not only housing).

This law adds to the list of classes protected under the federal law. It provides that it is illegal for any person to refuse to engage in or negotiate for a real estate transaction with a person because of sex, marital status, race, creed, color, national origin, families with children status, sexual orientation, honorably discharged veteran or military status, or the presence of any sensory, mental, or physical disability, or the use of a trained guide dog or service animal by a person with a disability.

Persons with **acquired immune deficiency syndrome** (AIDS), or persons who test positive for the **human immunodeficiency virus** (HIV) and other related medical conditions, are considered disabled under the state statute.

The state and local agencies that deal with fair housing issues in Washington include:

- Tacoma Human Services Division: www.cityoftacoma.org/government/city_departments/neighborhood_and_community_services/human_services_division/
- King County Office of Civil Rights: www.kingcounty.gov/exec/CivilRights.aspx
- Seattle Office for Civil Rights: www.seattle.gov/civilrights
- Fair Housing Center of Washington: www.fhcwashington.org/

Escrow Agents
[RCW 18.44]

In order to protect the public, the Escrow Agent Registration Act requires most persons engaging in the business of closing escrow to be registered by the Department of Financial Institutions. Licensed escrow persons are called **certified escrow agents**. In Washington, certain persons or entities may act as escrow agents without obtaining a certificate of registration, including:

- licensed attorneys while performing their professional duties
- persons acting under court order (e.g., receivers, trustees, executors, administrators, guardians)
- banks, trust companies, mutual savings banks, savings and loans associations, and credit unions
- insurance companies
- title insurance companies and their agents
- federally approved lending institutions and agencies
- real estate brokers who close transactions they have handled or negotiated, if they do not charge or receive compensation for escrow services

Brain Teaser 1

Complete the following sentences to reinforce your understanding of the material.

1. When homestead property is sold in order to acquire a new homestead, the exemption protects the sale proceeds and the new property for ___ year(s).
2. A claim of mechanic's lien must be filed within ___ day(s) after the work has ceased or materials have been delivered.
3. Unless a buyer waives the right to receive the disclosure statement, a seller must give him/her a disclosure statement within ___ business day(s) of acceptance of an offer to purchase a residential property, unless otherwise agreed.
4. Security deposit refunds must be delivered to the tenant within ___ day(s) after termination of the rental agreement and vacation of the premises.
5. The Washington law against discrimination has fewer exemptions than federal law. It applies to all types of _____, not only housing.

Brain Teaser Answers

Brain Teaser #1

1. When homestead property is sold in order to acquire a new homestead, the exemption protects the sale proceeds and the new property for <u>one</u> year.

2. A claim of mechanic's lien must be filed within <u>90</u> days after the work has ceased or materials have been delivered.

3. Unless a buyer waives the right to receive the disclosure statement, a seller must give him/her a disclosure statement within <u>five</u> business days of acceptance of an offer to purchase a residential property, unless otherwise agreed.

4. Security deposit refunds must be delivered to the tenant within <u>14</u> days after termination of the rental agreement and vacation of the premises.

5. The Washington law against discrimination has fewer exemptions than federal law. It applies to all types of <u>real estate</u>, not only housing.

Review — Washington Laws

This lesson reviews some specific state laws related to real property transactions. The lesson begins with water rights and community property and continues with taxes, construction liens, and foreclosures. This is followed by a discussion of the Residential Landlord-Tenant Act and leases. State laws addressing discrimination and escrow conclude the lesson.

State statute provides that water in Washington is considered to be owned by the general public. Therefore, a riparian owner (i.e., one who owns land along the bank of a river or stream) does not automatically have the right to use water. In order to be allowed to divert waters for private use, a landowner must obtain a water rights certificate from the Supervisor of Water Resources at the Department of Ecology.

Under state law, all real property in Washington and all personal property anywhere acquired by a husband and wife during a valid marriage or by persons in a state-registered domestic partnership is community property unless specifically acquired by one or the other as separate property. Either spouse or partner acting alone may manage and control community property without the consent of the other. But neither can encumber or sell community household goods, furnishings, or appliances without the other's signature; give away community property without the other's consent; or sell, convey, or encumber the community real property alone.

A homestead exemption may protect a homeowner from foreclosure on unsecured liens (i.e., judgments and other liens in which the property was not originally offered as security for the debt). It will not defeat foreclosure on secured liens, such as mortgages, deeds of trust, or homeowners or condominium association liens.

In Washington, the tax assessor determines what real and personal property is taxable, assesses it, and gets it listed on the tax rolls. In assessing the property, the assessor must determine its true value and fair value as of January 1, the assessment date. Property taxes become a lien on real property on the first day of the tax year, January 1. They remain a lien until paid. Taxes may be paid in two installments: half by April 30 and the other half by October 31.

An excise tax of 1.28% of the sales price (plus an additional amount added by local authorities) is imposed on the transfer of title to, or of an estate in, real property when valuable consideration is given.

Mechanics' liens and materialmen's liens are considered statutory liens, as state statute gives people who have furnished work or material for the improvement of real property the right to place a lien on that property if they are not paid. A claim of lien must be filed within 90 days after the work has ceased or materials have been delivered.

If a mortgagor defaults on the promises he/she makes in the note or mortgage, then the lender has the right to sue on the note to obtain a judgment or request that the property be foreclosed and sold through court action. A court foreclosure will wipe out the borrower's equitable right of redemption (i.e., the right to pay off the mortgage debt plus interest and costs prior to the foreclosure). Normally following a foreclosure the mortgagor has a new statutory right of redemption to pay off the amount of the judgment decree. This redemption period is one year, but it may be shortened or eliminated under certain circumstances.

A seller of commercial real estate or improved or unimproved residential real estate in Washington is required to give the buyer a complete seller disclosure statement, unless the buyer waives the right to receive the disclosure statement or the transfer is exempt from the requirement. The seller must disclose, based upon his/her personal knowledge, matters relating to title and condition of the property. Within three business days from receipt of the statement (or as otherwise agreed), the buyer may either approve and accept the statement or give written notice of rescission of the sales agreement.

The Residential Landlord-Tenant Act (the Act) applies to rentals of residences in homes, multiplexes, apartments, and mobile homes. It outlines the responsibilities of landlords and tenants. The landlord must keep the property fit for human habitation. His/Her responsibilities include maintaining the premises to comply with all state and local statutes and codes that affect the tenant's health and safety; maintaining all structural components; keeping common and shared areas clean and safe; maintaining all electrical, plumbing, heating, and other facilities he/she supplies; providing adequate heat, water, and hot water; and more. The Act also spells out the obligations of the tenant and provides remedies for landlords of tenants who do not meet those obligations.

The basic provisions of a residential lease include the term, provisions for termination, and the renewal of the lease with regard to rent, the amount, when and where it is payable, and when a late fee will be imposed and for what amount; the amount of security deposit and terms under which it is refundable; the purpose and amount of any nonrefundable fees; tenant responsibilities regarding use and maintenance of the premises; landlord responsibilities regarding provision of habitable premises; policies regarding pets, smoking, parking, etc.; and the landlord's right to access the premises.

Washington's law against discrimination (RCW 49.60) prohibits practices of discrimination by any person in a real estate transaction. This law adds to the list of classes protected under the federal law. It provides that it is illegal for any person to refuse to engage in or negotiate for a real estate transaction with a person because of sex; marital status; race; creed; color; national origin; families with children status; the presence of any sensory, mental, or physical disability, which includes HIV and AIDS, or the use of a trained guide dog or service animal by a person with a disability; sexual orientation; or honorably discharged veteran or military status.

In order to protect the public, the Escrow Agent Registration Act requires most persons engaging in the business of closing escrow to be registered by the Department of Financial Institutions. Licensed escrow persons are called "certified escrow agents." Certain persons or entities are exempt from registration requirements.

This concludes the review for Washington Laws.

Index

accounting 57
acquired immune deficiency syndrome
    (AIDS) 82
address changes, of offices 27
advertising 42–43, 65
affiliated licensees 9
agencies, for fair housing issues 82
Agency Agreement 43
AIDS (acquired immune deficiency
    syndrome) 82
appeals 35–36, 40
application, for license acquisition 17
appraisal 47
appraisers 2
assessed value 72
assistants, personal 11
Attorney General's Office 2, 36
attorneys 10, 36
audits 28

banking institution 50
beneficiary 76
blockbusting 46
branch manager 7, 9–10,
    21–22, 27, 29
branch offices 27
Brokerage Relationships Act
    agency agreement in 59
    agency terms in 62
    brain teasers on 63–64
    Brokerage Relationships
        Law in 59
    buyer in 58
    buyer's agent in 61, 67
    confidential information and 60
    disclosure in 59–60
    dual agent in 58, 61–62
    liability in 63, 67
    loyalty 60–61
    material fact in 59
    seller in 58
    seller's agent in 61, 67
Brokerage Relationships Law 59
brokerage service contracts 9

brokers 6, 8, 12, 21, 29
    See also designated brokers;
        licensees; managing brokers
brokers actively licensed in another
    jurisdiction 27–28, 34
broker's price opinion 6
business days 31
business entity 5
buyer 58, 61, 67

cease-and-desist orders 35–36
"certificate of sale," 75
certified escrow agents 83
character 14, 22, 34, 45
clock hours 14–15
closings 46
    of firm 30
collateral 74
commercial real estate 11–12
commingle 50, 53
the Commission. *See* Real Estate
    Commission
commissioners 4
commissions 46–47, 54, 65
communications, electronic 33
community property 70–71
community property agreement 70–71
competence, limiting activities
    to areas of 44–45
computer system, for records 54
conduct, general 45
confidential information 60
conflict of interest 4, 60
consensual lien 74
construction liens 73
continued 76
continuing education 13, 18–19
contractors 2
controlling interest 7
convert 50
crimes 59

declaration of forfeiture 77
deed of trust (DOT) 74–77

the Deed of Trust Act (1965) 76
default 74, 76, 81, 85
deficiency judgment 75
Department of Ecology 2
Department of Financial
    Institutions (DFI) 2, 48
Department of Labor and
    Industries 2
Department of Licensing (DOL) 2–4, 21
    firm names and 26
    licensed firm disclosure from 42
    short sales and 48
Department of Social and
    Health Services (DSHS) 45, 49
deposits 52, 57, 80
designated brokers 6–7, 21, 28–30
    records by 31–33, 40
    responsibilities of 8–9, 22, 31–33, 66
    trust account
        administration by 54–55, 66
DFI (Department of
    Financial Institutions) 2, 48
Director of Commerce 51
Director of the Department of
    Licensing (the Director) 3, 21, 29–32
    enforcement by 4, 34–36
disabilities 82
disbursements 57
    multi-party claims for 53
    in trust funds
        administration 52–54
disclosures 59–60, 78–79, 86
    from licensee 33, 40, 42–43
discrimination 46, 82, 86
DOL. *See* Department of Licensing
DOT (deed of trust) 74–77
DSHS (Department of Social
    and Health Services) 45, 49
dual agency 44–45
dual agent 58, 61–62

education 13–16, 18–19
electronic communications 33
enforcement
    Attorney General and 36
    cease-and-desist orders 35–36
    hearings and appeals 35–36, 40
    violations and sanctions 33–35, 40

enjoin the forfeiture 78
Environmental and Land Use
    Hearings Office 2
escrow 2
escrow agents 83
evictions 81
exam 14–16
excise tax 73, 85
exemptions 71–72, 85
    license requirement 10–11, 22
experience, license
    acquisition and 16–17

Fair Housing Act 82
fair housing issues 82
FDIC (Federal Deposit Insurance
    Corporation) 50
Federal Bureau of Investigation 14
Federal Deposit Insurance
    Corporation (FDIC) 50
fingerprinting 14, 18
firm (real estate firm) 5, 27
    brokers' licenses at 29, 39
    closing of 30
    disciplinary action against 28
    disclosures of 33
    enforcement and 33–36
    objectives related to 25
    overview of 25
    records of 28, 31–33
    review about 39–40
    trust funds to 49
    WCRER and 36–37
firm license 13, 18
firm requirements
    brain teaser on 31, 38
    inactive license 30, 39
    license maintenance
        and return 29–30
    names 26, 39
    offices 26–28
    supervision 28
foreclosure 85–86
    deed of trust and 76–77
    definition of 74
    forfeiture and 74–78
    judicial 75
    mortgage and 75–76

non-judicial 76–77
    promissory note and 74–75
forfeiture 77–78
franchisee names 26
fraudulent representation 34, 45
fulfillment deed 77
full-time experience 16
funds 31–33, 35

general conduct 45
good faith 61
grantors (trustors) 76
gross misdemeanor 34

hearings and appeals 35–36, 40
HIV (human immunodeficiency
    virus) 82
home inspector referrals 48
homestead 71–72
homestead exemption 71–72, 85
Housing Trust Fund 50–51, 64
human immunodeficiency
    virus (HIV) 82
Human Rights Commission 2, 21, 82

inactive licenses 30, 39
individual license renewal 18
injunction 36
interest 7, 50–52, 74
    conflict of 4, 60
interest-bearing trust account,
    separate 51–52
interim license 17, 22
internet advertising 42–43
intestate 71

judicial foreclosure 75
    non- 76–77
judicial sale 78

landlord obligations 79–80
    See also Residential
        Landlord-Tenant Act
law and regulations 1
    local regulation 2–3
    review of 21–23
    state real estate regulation 3
    state regulation 2–3

lease agreements 56
lease provisions 81–82, 86
liability 63, 67
license acquisition 19–20
    application for 17
    for brokers 12
    character and 14, 22
    clock hours related to 14–15
    education in 13–16
    exam for 14–17
    experience and 16–17
    for firm 13, 18
    for managing brokers 12–13
    prior licensure and 15
licensed firm disclosure 42
licensees 5, 7–10, 41
    brain teasers on 49, 63–64
    disclosures from 33, 40, 42–43
    out-of-state 11–12
    property management
        by 56–58, 66–67
    summary on 65–67
    trust funds administration
        by 49–55
licensee transactions 42–49
license expiration 17
license renewal 17, 23
    continuing education for 18–19
    for firm 18
    for inactive licenses 30
    for individual 18
    lateness in 19
license requirement 5–6, 12, 20
    commercial real estate 11
    exemptions 10–11, 22
    licensees' responsibilities 7–10
    personal assistants and 11
licenses
    inactive 30, 39
    at offices 26–27
    suspension of 45, 65
license termination 29–30, 35
license transfer 29
licensing, department of 3–4
liens 71, 73–74, 85
loan modifications 48
loans 2, 48, 73–76
loyalty 60–61

managing brokers 6, 8, 30
    license acquisition for 12–13
    responsibilities of 9–10, 22, 28–29
material fact 59
materialmen 74
materialmen's liens 74
mechanics' liens 74
misdemeanor, gross 34
mobile homes 47
mortgage 74
    foreclosure and 75–76
mortgage loan originator 2

names, firm 26, 39
National Credit Union
    Administration (NCUA) 50
natural person 5
NCUA (National Credit Union
    Administration) 50
non-judicial foreclosure 76–77
nonrefundable fees 80
Notice of Default 76
notice of intent to forfeit 77
Notice of Trustee's Sale 76

offers 43
Office of the Insurance
    Commissioner 2
out-of-state licensees 11–12

person, definition of 5
personal assistants 11
petition for judicial sale 78
pooled interest-bearing
    accounts 50–52
promissory note 74–75
property management
    agreement 56, 66
property management
    services 6, 10–11
    accounting in 57
    brain teasers on 58, 64
    deposits in 57
    disbursements in 57
    by licensees 56–58, 66–67
    property management trust
        accounts in 57
    summary statements in 56

property management
    trust accounts 57
property tax 72–73

RCW (Revised Code of Washington) 3
    See also specific topics
real estate broker. See brokers
real estate brokerage services 5–6
Real Estate Commission
    (the Commission) 4
    See also specific topics
real estate contract 9, 74
    forfeiture and 77–78
real estate firm. See firm
Real Estate Program.
    See specific topics
real estate transaction 58
real property transactions 69
    brain teasers on 83–84
    community property in 70–71
    construction liens in 73
    escrow agents in 83
    fair housing issues in 82
    foreclosure and forfeiture in 74–78
    homestead exemption in 71–72, 85
    residential landlords and
        tenants in 79–82
    seller's disclosure in 78–79, 86
    taxes in 72–73
    water rights in 70
records 37, 40, 54, 75
    of firm 28, 31–33
referrals 10, 47–48
rental agreements 56
Residential Landlord-Tenant Act 57
    defaults and evictions in 81
    deposits in 80
    landlord obligations in 79–80
    lease provisions in 81–82, 86
    nonrefundable fees 80
    tenant obligations in 81
Revised Code of Washington (RCW) 3
right of redemption 75, 77
riparian owner 70

sanctions 33–36, 40
security instrument 75
security interest 74

seller 58, 61, 67
seller's disclosure 78–79, 86
separate property 70
short sales/loan modifications 48
social media 42–43
state regulation 2–3
    See also specific topics
statutory liens 74
subagent 58
supervision, as firm requirement 28

tax assessor 72, 85
taxes 44, 72–73, 85
tenancy 44
    See also Residential
        Landlord-Tenant Act
title insurance 2
title insurance referrals 47–48
transactions
    advertising 42–43
    appraisal in 47
    brain teaser on 49
    closings in 46
    commissions in 46–47
    disclosures in 43
    discrimination in 46, 82, 86
    general conduct in 45
    home inspector referrals 48
    limiting activities to areas of
        competence in 44–45
    mobile homes in 47
    offers in 43
    short sales/loan modifications in 48
    title insurance referrals in 47–48
trial balance 55
trust account administration
    ledger sheets in 55
    reconciliation in 55
    system approval for 54

trust accounts 57
    options 51–52
    pooled interest-bearing
        accounts as 50–52
    records for 32–33
Trustee's Deed 76
trust funds administration 66
    brain teasers on 58, 64
    deposits in 52
    disbursements in 52–54
    by licensees 49–55
    other account options in 51–52
    trust account administration
        in 54–55
    trust accounts in 50–52
    trust funds in 49–50
trustors (grantors) 76

Unified Business Identifier
    (UBI) 6–7
unrepresented parties 44–45
unsecured liens 71

violations and sanctions 33–36

Washington Administrative
    Code (WAC) 3
    See also specific topics
Washington Center for Real
    Estate Research (WCRER) 36–37, 40
Washington State Human
    Rights Commission 82
Washington State Patrol
    Criminal Identification
    System 14
water rights 70, 85
WCRER (Washington Center
    for Real Estate Research) 36–37, 40
written agreements 61